The Voice of the ...

George Whitefield

The Voice that Woke the World

George Whitefield

Lucille Travis

CF4·K

10 9 8 7 6 5 4 3 2
Copyright © 2011 Lucille Travis
Reprinted in 2015
Paperback ISBN: 978-1-84550-772-5
Epub ISBN: 978-1-84550-881-4
Mobi ISBN: 978-1-84550-882-1

Published by
Christian Focus Publications,
Geanies House, Fearn, Ross-shire,
IV20 1TW, Scotland, U.K.
www.christianfocus.com
email: info@christianfocus.com

Cover design by Daniel van Straaten
Cover illustration by Brent Donoho
Printed and bound by Nørhaven, Denmark

The author has wherever it was possible tried to use Whitefield's words while quoting letters and diary entries. The dialogue and writings that are direct quotes from George Whitefield or based on these are written in italic.

All rights reserved. No part of this publication may be reproduced, stored in a retrieval system, or transmitted, in any form, by any means, electronic, mechanical, photocopying, recording or otherwise without the prior permission of the publisher or a licence permitting restricted copying. In the U.K. such licences are issued by the Copyright Licensing Agency, Saffron House, 6–10 Kirby Street, London, EC1 8TS. www.cla.co.uk

CHRISTIAN FOCUS PUBLICATIONS

Christian Focus | Christian Heritage | CF4K | Mentor

Christian Focus Publications publishes books for adults and children under its four main imprints: Christian Focus, CF4K, Mentor and Christian Heritage. Our books reflect our conviction that God's Word is reliable and Jesus is the way to know him, and live for ever with him.

Our children's publication list includes a Sunday School curriculum that covers pre-school to early teens, and puzzle and activity books. We also publish personal and family devotional titles, biographies and inspirational stories that children will love.

If you are looking for quality Bible teaching for children then we have an excellent range of Bible stories and age-specific theological books.

From pre-school board books to teenage apologetics, we have it covered!

Find us at our web page:
www.christianfocus.com

CF4•K
Because you're never
too young to know Jesus

Zach, we never dreamed of the fine grandson
God would give us in you.
The story of George Whitefield
is for all young people, like you,
who are facing a world once
more asleep to God.
Not Whitefield's voice or his skills,
but Whitefield's heart is the gift of God
I pray for you, and all of us.

The Boy from the Inn

George made his way along the market street through the crowds, horse drawn carts and impatient horsemen filling the cobblestone road. Smells of fish, leather and spices from the stalls mixed with the familiar foul smell of the ditch that ran along the street. Below on the Severn River he spotted a fishing vessel pulling into the dock. He liked to watch the boats at the wharf unload their wares for the City of Gloucester's markets, and there were always boats coming and going on the river.

The tobacco shop George was heading for stood close to the end of the market. There were no shortcuts to the small shop that stood wedged between other buildings behind the open market stalls. He had spotted the iron sign above the tobacco shop just as two boys who looked to be near his age, twelve or thirteen, came running from the entrance.

George flattened himself against the stone wall as the boys raced past and disappeared into the crowds of the noisy market. The stout, red-faced shopkeeper came running from the doorway shouting, "If I catch you in here again, I'll skin you alive." As the boys melted into the crowds he stopped and wiped his face on the corner of his apron. "Thieves," he muttered, turning back to the shop. George followed him inside.

The owner straightened a toppled box before he looked up. "Ah, it's you, young master Whitefield. You saw those two thieves? They'll be hanging from the gallows one of these days." He wiped his face once more. "Thanks be for them as brings their children up to be decent citizens like yourself. What can I do for you today, young sir?"

George smiled as he fingered the two coins he had stolen only that very morning from his mother's apron while she slept. She would never send him, the last born of her six sons to the gallows even though now in 1727, England's harsh code of law hanged thieves his age and younger. "Just a bit of tobacco for one of the guests," he said and smiled again, knowing that the guest did not exist.

He was nearly back to the inn when he passed a narrow alley and saw the same boys who had run from the tobacco shop. They were examining what looked like a shiny new smoking pipe. The taller boy saw George looking their way, and quickly stuck the pipe in the pocket of his oversized coat. "What ya' lookin' at, Squint Eyes? Go on. Get home to your mam and your fancy tavern."

"Yeah, Squint Eyes, fancy boy Squint Eyes," the younger boy chanted.

George looked away as if he hadn't heard them. He walked on until he had turned a corner out of their sight, and ran to the side street that would lead him to the inn and safety. 'Squint Eyes' the hated nickname burned in his heart. He wasn't cross-eyed. Only one eye squinted a bit from measles he'd had as a baby. "May God blast them!" The words of the Psalms calling down judgment on the wicked came to him quickly, and he would have thought of more if his sister Elizabeth had not called his name.

She was just coming from the entrance to the stables behind the great inn. "George Whitefield, where have you been?" Her blue eyes snapped, and her wheat colored hair that was so like his, stuck out from under her cap. The broom in her hand told George she had been at work. "You'd better not let old toad Longden catch you." It was the name she always called their stepfather. "Everyone is hurrying around trying to stay out of his way. Have you forgotten that tonight the players are coming and the whole inn is full?"

George glanced up at the Bell Inn. It was three stories high and the finest in Gloucester; at least it had been when his father was still alive. "I haven't forgotten," George said. "The play is well enough and the players, but with our stepfather running things, you know there won't be any profit this night. He's ruining the inn and everyone knows it," George said.

Elizabeth was one year older than George and already like their mother. Her eyes filled with tears now as she stood searching her brother's face. Their older brothers were always kept busy under the heavy hand of their stepfather, but she and George still managed to share most things together. "George, you were only two years old when our father died and you don't remember him. He was a good father and a good husband. I'm worried about our mother more than the Inn." She lowered her voice, "I do not think she will be married much longer to Longden."

George nodded his head. "It's worse than I thought then. But the sooner that man is gone the better. I will leave school and see what I can do to help our mother with the work. It may be we can yet keep the Bell Inn." With a pat on Elizabeth's shoulder, George went quickly through the back entrance. Though he would miss the wildness and mischief with his friends he wouldn't mind leaving school. At least tonight he would get to see one of the plays he so loved, even though he must watch it from his special hiding place.

That night as George watched the actors in their splendid costumes perform on stage he quietly mouthed his favorite lines. He was good at imitating the actor's voices. Each year at St. Mary's de Crypt school he was the one chosen to perform before important visitors. He loved acting and one of his favorite roles was to be a minister. He especially liked pretending to be the local clergyman, an older gentleman giving a sermon or reading prayers. He might even like to be a real clergyman some day. He would be good at it, and ministers of the Church of England enjoyed respect and honor, and could make a good living. They were also free to enjoy whatever pleasures of English society they liked, including plays. Freedom was not something George enjoyed these days. The heavy hand of his stepfather made everyone fearful and angry. As George thought of his stepfather, he missed the words on stage that made the audience suddenly burst into laughter.

True to his word, George begged his mother to let him leave school and help at the inn. Tearfully, she agreed. "You'll need this," she said handing him a large blue apron. At once George put it on and from then on wore it as he served customers at the tap.

As the weeks passed George became a well-known face behind the bar. Many of his patrons were already drunk as they called out for refills. George and his friends had once or twice become drunk, and happily they had not been found out. Now he must mop up after drunken guests, clean rooms, and help with whatever customers demanded. At night in his room he studied plays and read books. Now he wished he were back at school learning the classics. He also missed his former friends and the rowdy life they had enjoyed together. He had no time for it now. He was good at what he did in the inn, but things had only gotten worse under his stepfather's greed and mismanagement. And to make things worse his mother and Elizabeth were no longer at home. George's mother had left her husband and the inn to live in a small place much poorer than what she had once had. She had taken Elizabeth with her.

Tired as he was, George's one joy was to read each night, and when he could he helped himself to books from their unsuspecting owners. Often they were devotional books like the book he was reading this night. The candle on the table in front of him had worn down to a stub when someone knocked on his door. "It's me, Richard," said a low voice.

As his older brother Richard entered the room George noted the tired lines on his face, but there was also a look he hadn't seen lately: a determined one. Their stepfather had not only stolen the inn away from them; he had turned Richard into a servant to whom he showed no mercy. Richard sat on the edge of George's cot. "You need to know that Longden has left in a rage," he said. "The court has ruled in my favor and the Inn is now in my hands."

George stood so quickly he nearly upset his table. "Brother, this is good news! Does our mother know?"

"She knows," Richard replied. "And there's more that will surprise even you, George. I have married a wife and she will now be mistress of this Inn. I have no doubt that you will find the place much changed for the better and soon. We shall one day have the Bell back to her old greatness, eh brother?"

George's head spun with all the news. When his brother had gone and closed the door behind him, George smiled. He wouldn't mind working hard at the inn now that it was back in the family. He would sleep well tonight. His dreams were untroubled and morning came brightly, but with it trouble quickly returned.

His new sister-in law, a tall, commanding woman, soon let George know that she wanted him gone. Nothing George did seemed to please her. If he started the cleaning at one end, she would say he should have started at the other. They fought continually and by the end of a month they were no longer speaking to each other.

Before the year was out George could stand it no longer, and left to visit a brother living in Bristol. He did not know if he would return to the inn or not. One Sunday with his brother's family at the church of St. John the sermon of the day seemed meant just for him. As he listened he told himself, "I shall never go back to a life of serving in a tavern." He would mend his ways, and stay away from his wild friends.

Back in Gloucester, George stayed with his mother and Elizabeth in their cramped quarters. His mother had once known a comfortable life and came from a good family. Now she wore old gowns, and they lived on very little money. George tried but could not find work he was willing to do. At night his mother would sit sewing by candlelight as George read and wrote. Often she would say, "George, if only you could go to Oxford and study. I always hoped you would be a minister, son." George would nod his head and say,

"I would love to go, Mother, but there is no money for Oxford."

One day everything changed. He had just entered the house when an excited Elizabeth, her face warm from the cooking fire, blurted out some news, "George, your friend Henry came to visit this very day and he's left word for you with our mother. Come sit down, you must hear this."

Puzzled, George sat at the table as his mother laid a paper before him. "Henry has left a note to tell you how you may go free to Oxford to become a minister. Think of the high honor you will bring our family, son as a minister!"

George read Henry's note. "He says servitors work as servants and are allowed to take courses for free. Students from wealthy families will pay fees to a servitor to shine boots, carry books, clean rooms – whatever the rich students want done. He says I may apply to be a servitor at Pembroke College, one of the colleges at Oxford. Mother, I would like to do this," George said.

"You must go back to St. Mary's school with your old Master and finish your studies of the classics," his mother said. "You'll need those to enter Oxford."

George could feel his heart beating loudly as he faced his old Master at St. Mary's school. "Yes, Sir, I want to enter the church and serve God." Would the Master believe him? In the past George had often entertained the other students by mocking the clergy? George waited for his answer.

"Perhaps there is more to you, young Whitefield, than ever I thought," the Master said. "Does that head of yours still recall its Latin?" Opening a book and handing it to George, he ordered him to read. As George began to read the page its Latin words came easily to his tongue. "That will do," the Master said. "We shall prepare you for Oxford. The rest is up to you and God."

George smiled. He was certain he could do this. Already he could tell a story as well as the local parish priest! He had even written sermons to amuse his friends.

The Servitor and the Methodists

The church was cold in spite of the early morning winter sun. A handful of people, mostly old folks, sat in the pews ahead of George listening to the prayers being read. The words, "Be merciful to me a sinner," rang so loudly in George's ears and heart that he stopped listening to the rest of the prayers. He needed mercy, and he was a sinner! He was back to his old ways. He hadn't returned to school long, before he joined his schoolmates in a life that had nothing to do with school. He and his friends were known in town as rakes, fashionable young men who lived wildly, sometimes doing shameful things. If the schoolmaster found out, he would be more than just displeased. He might expel George. How could he go to Oxford and become a minister? He covered his face, and said the words over and over, "O God, be merciful to me a sinner."

When at last he looked up, the December sun streaming in the window bathed him in its light. Was it a sign that God had heard his pleas? "I will be back for evening prayers," he vowed.

He returned home that evening eager to please God. George flew up the stairs and into the apartment

17

where his mother sat sewing by the fire. Elizabeth stood stirring the large cooking pot and George patted her shoulder as he passed. "What was that for?" she asked. "Don't tell me you're invited to some big party while I'm stuck here slaving away!" George just grinned.

His mother raised her face for his greeting, with the smile she always kept for him. "Mother," he said, "I'll be seventeen this 16th December. I will prepare myself to take the holy sacrament on Christmas Day, and this night I will begin to read devotional books again. I have been to public worship twice today, and intend to keep it up." The look of astonishment on his mother's face delighted George. "Yes, Mother, it's your very own son George you see before you. I believe God wants me to be a minister like you hoped."

Elizabeth had stopped tending the stew to listen. "Well, if God wants it you had better get on with it, but I'll believe it when I see it." She laughed and returned to stirring the supper stew.

First, George needed to confess to the schoolmaster that he and his friends had broken the Master's rules for Christian behavior, and he was truly sorry. The Master's stern discipline fell on them all, but to George it seemed almost welcome. He studied hard and this time he did not go with his friends who soon went back to their old ways.

Not only his mother, but Elizabeth and his brothers were amazed when one year later they stood waving farewell to an excited George on his way to the university. He had changed!

His arrival at Pembroke College, a massive stone building, one of Oxford's several colleges, nearly took his breath away. It seemed to George like sacred ground, the place that held the key to all he dreamed of becoming. However, life at Oxford was not the same for all its students. George stood in the garret dorm room high up under the roof. This was the place where the lowliest of all students lived, the servitors who would receive free tuition at Oxford for their service. The room was unheated and poorly furnished. It would be George's quarters for the next three years.

Like all the servitors George put on the plain robe that marked him as a servant. Students of a higher rank wore finer robes and did not talk to servitors other than to give orders. A servitor was not allowed to speak to those above his station other than to answer his own master. Servitors had their own discussions in philosophy and not with the rest of the students. When the entire college took the Holy Sacrament, servitors took it on another day just for them.

Thankfully, George soon had a friend — round faced, jolly Marcus, a servitor like himself and one of his room-mates. Before the first day was over George was called to serve three gentlemen. He would receive some money, and the gift of an occasional book or cast off clothing.

By the end of a week blacking shoes, straightening rooms, running errands, waking them in the mornings, and doing assignments for two of them, George was in high demand. George found that his duties were much like those he had done at the inn, and he was good at them. However, there was one duty he wasn't happy about. A servitor had to check his gentlemen's rooms at night to see if they were there and report to the Master of the college any who were not. It made George feel awkward, and he hoped he would never have to report on any of them. Meanwhile his education had started and George's tutor was not only a learned man, but a kind one willing to help George learn. Already the tutor had lent him a book to study.

George sat reading one evening in the light of his candle on a propped up table. As usual the attic room was cold and George shivered. All four of his room-mates were gone out in search of warmth and mirth in a local alehouse. A small stab of fear pinched George's insides when he thought of his own past living for pleasures. He knew how quickly drinking and partying could become a way of life dangerous to all his hopes and dreams. Marcus and the others had laughed at him earlier when he refused to go with them, but he dared not go back to his old ways even if it meant being alone in a freezing room.

As George turned a page the door opened, and Marcus stuck his head in. "Change your mind yet, old fellow? I've enough for a pint for both of us tonight and you can pay me back next week." Marcus' round face seemed always merry and ready for a good time. "Well?" he asked.

George shook his head. "You know I have no love for taverns," he said. "It's kind of you, Marcus, but I need to study."

"Suit yourself, then. You'll freeze in here. Don't say I didn't warn you." Marcus shut the door and silence settled back into the room, a cold silence. George grew so cold he could not get warm and barely slept that night. But before he knew it winter days had turned into spring, and something new came into George's life.

George lifted his face to the warm sun as he and Marcus walked together from the noon meal they had eaten with the other servitors. "There goes one of those Methodist fellows," Marcus said. Marcus was looking in the direction of an upperclassman hurrying towards the gate with a Bible under his arm. "There's to be a public hanging tomorrow and I wager he's on his way to visit the fellow in the condemned hole."

George nodded. "If that's where he goes, then I say God be with him. I've visited prisoners in Newgate, and the place is filthy, no fireplace, and an open sewer running through it. The rats are a menace. The prisoners are all thrown together whether they're young or old, hardened criminals or the least offenders. I've seen poor women with their small children, some of them in prison just for stealing food to keep alive."

"Not a place I'd want to visit." Marcus said. "I know you've been working among the poor, reading to them, visiting the sick, going to church, even taking the sacrament every week," Marcus said. "Some of us think you are carrying things a bit too far. There's a rumor that your own tutor thinks so too. Better watch out, or they'll be calling you a Methodist."

George felt his face grow warm. Secretly, he admired the small group of young Oxford students called Methodists. Like everyone else at Oxford they belonged to the Church of England, but were called Methodists by those who mocked them. They were known for their kindness, their good works, and the strict, disciplined way they lived. Each kept a journal of how he spent every hour of the day striving to please God, noting the good works he'd done that day. They met regularly in one or another's rooms to study and pray together. George longed to know them, but as a servitor he dared not introduce himself to them. He could however, defend them.

"They are good men, Methodists or not," George insisted. "And I know what my own tutor thinks of me, but he is still willing to loan me books and teach me. I think him the kindest of men."

"So long as you don't hang around with the Methodists, old fellow, I'm sure you will be okay," Marcus said.

The following day George did more than hang around with the despised group.

He had finished his morning duties for the gentlemen he served and now hurried away from Pembroke. He'd received a note at the six a.m. reading of prayers for an invitation to breakfast with one of the Methodists and an upperclassman! Swallowing hard George knocked on the door of Charles Wesley, brother of John Wesley, a leader of the Methodist group. Charles opened the door himself. He was not tall, not as tall as George, but he seemed dignified yet gentle, and the look on his face was a kind one. "Come in, Mr. Whitefield. I've been expecting you, come have some breakfast."

Seated together at the table Charles prayed the grace and then served George's plate. "Now, I know that as a servitor you could not have come to us," he said handing him the platter, "and so we have taken the liberty of coming to you, sir. My brother John and I have noticed your faithful attendance at church and we've seen and heard about the good works you have been doing. We felt we needed to meet you face to face."

When breakfast was over and George left he carried a book kindly lent to him by Charles Wesley. There would be others, many of them, and George would indeed be known as one of those "Methodists" in the Holy Club.

Each night now, George wrote the day's events carefully into his journal. His new purpose was to waste no part of the day, but to do all he could to live a disciplined life as a member of the Holy Club.

Weeks went by and Marcus no longer bothered to invite George to go out with the rest of his roommates. Tonight was no different. The last one to leave, Marcus stood in the doorway looking at George. "Just tell me how giving up every pleasure is going to help you once you finish Oxford?" he asked.

George looked up from the new devotional book he was reading. "Well, Marcus, for one thing I hope to have a quiet little English parish where I can live a disciplined life and teach my congregation to do the same. We need to make every effort we can to live rightly. Don't you fear God, Marcus?

Marcus laughed. "No," he said, "I do not fear God, and I am sure he is no more interested in me or any of us than the King is in some poor creature living somewhere in a corner of the kingdom. However, I agree with you on the quiet little English church so long as it comes with a good living." Marcus smiled at George. "You know that all the people want from a minister in the Church of England is that he follow the rituals and rules of the Church and be a pleasant fellow. So long as he is not too religious everyone is happy." Laughing, Marcus left before George could answer.

George wanted to call out after him, "But to be a Christian a man must live a strict life of good works and self-denial, as well as go to church, say his prayers, and receive the sacrament." George closed the book in front of him. Marcus was wrong. No one could be too religious. No one could do too many good works.

Maybe he needed to do more. Tomorrow he would skip buying fruit and take the money to the first poor family he visited.

Word spread quickly that Whitefield was now a Methodist. Some of his fellow servitors pelted his clean robe with dirt. The gentlemen who employed George now thought him fair game for fun, and some kept back the money they owed for his services. In class some teachers mocked Methodists. George tried to ignore the taunts. He visited the sick and the poor and told himself it was a Christian's duty to be kind and not waste a single hour.

Burn the Book, throw it down, or search it?

The Master of the college looked grim as he said, "Whitefield, all this visiting the sick and the poor has to stop. I will not tolerate such goings on from any of our students, and that includes servitors such as you. You are here at Oxford to study and learn in a dignified manner." The Master's face and voice left no doubt that he was truly angry.

George felt his face redden, and quickly said, "I understand, Sir."

"See that you do. That will be all, Whitefield."

Dismissed, George quietly left the room. He hadn't said he agreed with the Master, only that he understood. How could he stop doing what the Bible so clearly commanded, like visiting the sick? The buildings they lived in were old, dirty, foul places, many with windows patched with black paper or rags. People there were often sick with fevers. He felt the small bag of money he'd saved from his food money. Some poor family would benefit from it. However, it would not go far.

As he hurried down the street someone called his name. It was Charles Wesley. "George, I've been looking for you." Charles held out a book. "I haven't read this yet, but I thought you might like to borrow it while I'm away this week."

George glanced at the title before he tucked the book into his robe, *The Life of God in the Soul of Man*, by Henry Scougal. What in the world does that mean? George wondered. "This one should make me think. Thanks, Charles."

It was late when George started to read the book. The title puzzled him. He had no idea what it meant. His first candle burned down, and then another as he went on reading. "If this book belonged to me, I would burn it or at least throw it away," he told himself as he finished. It is a dreadful thing to read that anyone may go to church, say his prayers, and receive the sacrament, but not be a Christian. George closed the book and began arguing with himself. It's true some like Marcus do these things because they are supposed to do them, not because they care about them. But I believe we must do them all to please God and as many good works as we can. How can this book say you may do them all earnestly and not be a Christian? What does it mean that a Christian must have God's life inside him? He could not help opening the book again.

This time as he finished a long shudder went through him. "Lord, God, if I am not a Christian, or if I am not a real one, for Jesus' sake show me what Christianity is so that I won't end my life lost forever." For a long while he sat thinking what the writer of the book meant by saying "Christ must be formed in us."

How could he, George Whitefield, make that happen? He'd read of saints who tried to commune with God by giving up all worldly things for a life of prayer and strict discipline. Was that the way? At the sounds of loud laughter in the hall, he snuffed out the candle and hurried to his bed. With his face to the wall he pretended sleep. The room was soon filled with his room-mates back from the alehouse. The smell of gin hung in the air, along with curses as they stumbled to their beds. George lay awake. Tomorrow he would fast, and pray.

Days turned into weeks and George could think of nothing but the words of the little book. How could he find such closeness to God? He must follow the example of those saints he'd read about. He would deny himself all but the poorest foods, the poorest clothes, even friends. He stopped going to meetings of the Holy Club. He did not attend his tutor's lectures, and burst into tears when his kindly tutor came to see him. "I cannot come, cannot think or do the lessons at this time," he tried to explain.

His tutor shook his head. "Yes, I can see that you can't. But this must stop or you will be expelled and there is little I can do for you."

More weeks passed and George did not return to the Holy Club. Charles had come to see him. "Look at yourself, George. This is not like you." His face was gentle. "You need to rest, and let us care for you," he said.

"You mean well, "George said, "but I am not mad as you seem to think. When I have come to the end of my search you will see. The way may be hard, but it's the only way for me. I must go on. You will see." Charles finally left, and George went back to the latest devotional book he was reading.

He no longer read any other books. If a devotional book said one should speak but little, he decided not to speak at all unless truly necessary, not even in prayer. During the six weeks of Lent he ate only a little coarse bread and drank sage tea for his meals. He was eating his small meal in his room when Marcus came in, and threw his books on the floor near his bed. "You look sick. You don't eat enough to keep going. All this fasting just makes you paler than death." Marcus shook his head and left, banging the door closed behind him.

George felt both weary and dizzy. He looked down at his hands and wrists. He had grown thin. He could barely pray and he no longer felt able to think about what he read and had stopped trying. Slowly he pushed away from the table. "I can't give up now." Maybe the end was near and God would accept his suffering as enough, and draw him close to himself. He would know when it came, some mystical feeling that would come to him from God's presence. That had to be what the little book meant.

He had made the climb down from the garret and managed to go as far as the gardens where he kneeled on the cold ground to pray. Nothing happened, not even when he lay flat, face down. He bore the cold as long as he could, and with the little strength left in him made his way back to the bottom of the stairs to his attic room. It was as far as he got. He collapsed on the second step too ill to move.

"Whitefield, are you sick?" The servitor who stood over him shook his shoulder, and George tried to speak but it was too much effort. "It's me, Hugh, and I think you need help." Hugh had often fallen down from too much ale, but not in the daytime like this. Besides, his room-mate looked utterly pale. Was he dying? "Help, I need help over here, help," he shouted. Soon others came and together they carried George up to his bed. Someone ran to fetch his tutor, and soon both the tutor and a doctor were bending over a half-conscious George.

The portly doctor finished examining George and shook his head. "This young man must stay put in that bed for the next six weeks. Good food and rest, sir, and we may have you up on your feet." He turned to the tutor. "I believe he will need far longer than six weeks in bed to truly recover, more like months back in his home to rest and let his mind and body grow stronger. Such foolish mistreatment of the body! I've seen this kind of thing turn into complete madness and death. It's well we've caught him in time."

George lay in his bed totally exhausted and sick. He closed his eyes. He could not get up if he tried. The days spent in bed went by slowly. Marcus kindly brought him his New Testament and a devotional book to read, but George was often too weak to read long. Occasionally Marcus brought him fruit. Today he handed George an apple. "You better eat this," he said. "You're thin as a rail. Why don't you forget all this religion? Once you get back on your feet and graduate, you'll get a church living and you won't need any of this." George thanked him for his kindness and waited for Marcus to leave before he began reading again.

By the end of his weeks in bed George had improved some, but inside he felt empty and defeated. Marcus was right. He had made himself deathly sick, and all for nothing. He'd tried as hard as he could to be worthy of God, but he felt no closer to him. Alone in the room and miserable, he bowed his head. "Lord God, it's no use, I can only throw myself on your mercy. Save me, Lord." His throat was dry and he longed for water.

As if light had come to fill a dark room, he remembered Jesus saying, "I thirst," when he was dying on the cross for our sins, and then Jesus had said, "It is finished!" George felt like a blind man who has just been healed and can suddenly see! On the cross the Lord Jesus had done the work of saving him, and it was finished! He thought of the Bible verse: "To all who received him, who believed in his name, Jesus gave the right to become children of God."

"I see it," George cried. "I tried so hard to save myself, but all my good deeds and rule keeping didn't save me, you did, Lord! God makes us his children when we receive you and believe in your name." George bowed his head. "I never understood what it meant when you told Nicodemus in the Bible that he must be born again, but I see it, Lord. No one can work their way into your family, we must be born into it. It's a new birth into God's family when we receive you, and believe in your name."When Marcus entered the room George threw his arms around his shoulders and cried, "Marcus, dear friend, there's hope for us, for all of England, the whole Church of England, and it's all in the new birth." George practically danced with joy, and Marcus had no choice but to listen to this strange thing George called "the new birth."

At first Marcus's round face had a puzzled look mixed with a bit of fear. It seemed like a new George standing before him talking about what God had done for him. It was certainly not the old George. How long they talked Marcus didn't know, or when he began to feel as though a heavy burden rolled off his back.

"I haven't told anyone this," Marcus said, "but living for a good time and planning to take a church job for the honor that comes with it, and the money, didn't make me feel good inside. Now I know what's been missing all along." Marcus put his head in his hands. "God is who I need. Will you pray for me, George?"

With tears running down his face, George put his arm about Marcus's shoulder. "With all my heart," he said. George prayed, and then Marcus. "The Lord will never let go of us, Marcus. Welcome to the family of God! This calls for a celebration," George said, "and I know just the small shop where we can find good wholesome food, and I am truly hungry!" For the first time in months George's appetite was back.

Happy as he felt George had not fully recovered from his close brush with death, and quickly tired even after so many weeks in bed. When his tutor said, "You must go home for a good rest away from studies for awhile," George agreed.

He wrote to the family that he was coming, and told them the good news of what God had done for him. An answering note came back quickly from his brother Richard. "Are you mad? Too much religion and too much pious talk isn't good for you," he wrote. "What you need is a good rest and a heavy dose of fresh old English countryside."

George smiled as he read Richard's note. At least he was right about the rest and the fresh old English countryside.

A New Fire

From the coach window George watched as they drove past the familiar streets and buildings of Gloucester, his boyhood home. His brother Richard, his sister Elizabeth and his boyhood friend, red haired Gabriel Harris stood at the coach stop waiting for him.

Gabriel looked taller, but wore the same old good-natured grin on his face.

George's legs wobbled a bit when he stepped down from the coach. It had been a rough trip, and he was still not strong. "Steady there, old boy," Gabriel said and grasped his arm. "George, you are staying with us, and we won't take no for an answer. My father is still the mayor here, and I am Younger Sheriff, so you'll just come with us." Gabriel laughed. "Besides, Mother can't wait to nurse you back to health and we've plenty of room." George smiled and nodded. He could hardly refuse.

Mrs. Harris, round and cheerful rushed to embrace George. He was soon seated in a great high-backed chair with his feet on a stool, pillows at his back, and blankets tucked about him. The smell of pine logs blazing in the great fireplace, and its warmth, soothed George's weary body. He didn't notice when his eyes closed and he fell asleep. Hours later Elizabeth entered the room with a full supper tray and woke him.

"Mrs. Harris didn't have the heart to wake you, but she insisted I stay and care for you this evening." Carefully Elizabeth set the tray on a table by George's chair. "I am longing to hear everything about Oxford, all that's been going on," she said. "Our mother is pleased you are home." Elizabeth handed George a napkin. "But, she is not so pleased about what you've been writing in your letters. Neither of us knows what you mean by this 'new birth'. Mother thinks you say these things because you have been working too hard, and become ill."

George smiled at his only sister. She had grown into a young woman. "If you will wait until I finish this good supper, I will tell you of the best news you or anyone will ever hear."

As she listened Elizabeth was astounded. "All my life I've heard that belonging to the church and doing good works means you are a Christian," she said, "now I begin to see it is a gift from God through Jesus. But why have we never heard of this in church?" George looked tired, and Elizabeth quickly said, "Never mind. You've talked enough for tonight." Picking up the supper tray she said, "You, little brother, need to go to bed."

George longed to tell everyone he could the good news, but first he needed to get his strength back. While he rested he studied the Bible. It was easiest to spread out his Bible, his Greek New Testament, and his Matthew Henry Commentary before him on the floor and study on his knees. "How wonderful your word is, dear Lord," he would whisper over a text that moved his heart.

One evening as George visited with his friend Gabriel he said, "Now that I have the truth to preach I can hardly wait to enter the ministry."

Gabriel smiled. "You may have to wait just a bit. You are only twenty years old and you will first have to be ordained to Holy Orders."

"Yes," George said, "and after that more work at Oxford until I can be ordained a priest in the Church of England. If this is God's will, he will make it possible."

Mrs. Harris was at last persuaded that George was well enough to receive friends. The young man who followed Mrs. Harris into the parlor where George reclined in a great chair near the fire was an old school friend. He wore a fine suit with silk ruffles on his cuffs, embroidery on his hose, silver buckles on his shoes, and carried a hat with more sweeping feathers on it than some birds had. It was clothing George knew well from his own wild days, the unmistakable style of a rake. Rakes were known for their love of fashion and love of pleasure, much of it immoral. George held out his hand and smiled. "Harry, it's been a long while since I've seen you. Sit down."

Bowing slightly to Mrs. Harris, Harry sat down. Mrs. Harris left the two of them together. "Well, well,

George, what's this I hear about your new choice of sermon? I remember how you used to imitate old Dr. Clary's sermons until the rest of us could scarcely breathe for laughing. You were good, George. I expect once you are a clergyman you will be quite the actor." He smiled at George. "But, come now that is not why I'm here. The boys and I can't wait to see you up and around. We plan a grand party for you: girls, wine, and perhaps a game or two of cards. So what can we do to hurry your recovery and have you back with us? Even a clergyman has a life when he's not in church." Harry chuckled.

George felt his heart sink. "No, Harry. I don't have a new sermon; I have a new life." As George told his old friend how his life had changed, and how he now considered his past ways sinful, he could see a dark shadow come over Harry's face.

Finally Harry rose and picked up his hat. "You have become a fanatic, George. I did not think the rumors about you were true, but I see that they are indeed so. Well, I must be going." With a half-bow Harry turned and left the room.

"If only I could have reached him, Lord," George prayed. "Young men like him need you. Help me bring your gift of hope to them, Lord."

In the months that followed, George did lead a group of young people to the Lord. The group met for prayer and Bible reading together at Elizabeth's home. She was now a married woman and opened her house gladly to the youths. George had also begun to do more of the things he loved to do like visiting the poor, and reading to the sick. One old woman came to trust in Jesus as her Savior only days before her death. George went to her funeral thinking how glad she must be now, in heaven with Jesus. He still kept a daily journal to record how he spent each day, but there were no more words of fear and gloom. "Ah, Lord, it is so good to tell you everything. You forgive me, you help me, and you never stop loving us" he wrote in his diary.

In the town of Gloucester where he had been born and raised, people were now saying things like, "He's a different lad than he used to be." Storekeepers, merchants, his old teacher, and pastor, friends he'd read plays with, everyone who knew him wondered at the change. "He goes to church more than any young man I've ever seen. Takes the sacrament weekly," the baker told his customers.

"I know he's been a-visitin' sick folk, and a-helpin' the poor too," the apple woman said. George surprised some people even more when he returned the books he had taken without their permission.

Lady Selwyn, a wealthy woman of Gloucester, was also impressed by Whitefield. She was a great friend of the Bishop of Gloucester, and while having tea in his parlor declared, "Now, dear Bishop, I know this extraordinary young man has just turned twenty one, but truly he is a remarkable young man and ought to be ordained. I for one, and there are many who agree with me, wish to see him here in a parish in Gloucester. What do you think, Bishop?"

"Indeed, your ladyship. I have been hearing much about this Whitefield," the Bishop replied, "and I believe your ladyship is quite right. I shall have a word with him, madam."

George wondered why the Bishop wanted to see him. By the time the meeting was over, he had kindly offered to ordain George as soon as he felt ready. Suddenly George felt too young, too small, too unworthy to take on such a task.

"You must trust God for the future, young man," the Bishop said, "and take the first step, my son."

On the day of his ordination George walked slowly up the steps of the great Gloucester Cathedral with its soaring towers and massive stone work. He could feel his heart thumping. As he opened the massive door of the church and entered, he breathed in the rich smell of incense and candles burning. Bishop Benson stood ready to begin the ceremony that would bring him into Holy Orders. As the congregation of witnesses watched George was ordained.

On Sunday he was to preach his first sermon at St. Mary's de Crypt, the church he'd gone to as a boy. The people were waiting; the same people who had known him all his life. As he walked to the pulpit he heard someone say, "He's terrible young, isn't he? Don't believe he'll have much to say to us, will he now?"

As George began to preach he no longer thought of anything but the message God had laid on his heart. By the end of the service a hush hung over the church. As he made his way down from the pulpit someone said, "Twas surely like the voice of an angel we heard." "And him so young," another said.

"Will you go back to Oxford and finish your studies?" Elizabeth asked George as the two walked from the church. "You will make a fine preacher, brother, and you will also make our old mother the proudest, happiest mother in Gloucester." She laughed lightly as George chuckled.

"I've already told God that if he wants me to go back to school I'm ready," he said opening the gate to the house.

Mrs. Harris beamed as she added still another letter to the pile in George's hands. "Now I confess I know what is inside some of these," she said. "I'm thinking you will be leaving us soon. And when you come back it will be to a church of your own." The letters contained money for George to return to Oxford, gifts from family, friends, and even the Bishop of Gloucester!

The last letter in George's hand was from a wealthy man in London, Sir John Phelps. "He is willing to provide a stipend for me to head the Holy Club Society work while I continue my studies at Oxford." George waved the letter. "This is more than I could have asked. I must make arrangements right away." Later that night George thought about what waited for him at Oxford. The Master of the College had been glad to see him go, and would not be glad to see him returning.

The Voice that Awakened England

George was right! The Master was not pleased to see him return to Oxford. On the day of his final exam George wished he had studied even later the night before. The test would cover every field of his studies at Oxford, and he must answer each question. "Pray for me, Marcus," he said as they came to the exam room.

An unsmiling Master and a large number of tutors and upper classmen were waiting for him. Sweat ran down George's neck into his robe as he concentrated on each question thrown at him. At the end the Master's stern voice pronounced that George Whitefield had passed the exam and was now ready to begin graduate work. Marcus pummeled George's shoulder. "Congratulations, brother, at last you can enjoy life at Oxford, do your studying, and lead the Holy Club too."

George smiled broadly. "I can't say I'm disappointed to be rid of my old life as a servitor." But all too soon he faced a new challenge. One of George's friends was a minister at the Tower of London Chapel who hoped to take a break while he finished his work at Oxford for a few months. He needed a replacement and asked George if he could help. George immediately said,

"I'm afraid I'd need two years more at Oxford and a hundred more sermons before I'd dare minister in such a large chapel." A week later he was on his way to the Tower of London Chapel.

"Awake this city to you, Lord Jesus," he prayed as he stepped from the coach. The London slums where the poor lived were filthy, crime ridden, foul smelling, terrible places. In another part of London the wealthy lived lives of indulgence and pleasure in grand homes. The Church of England's ministers enjoyed the luxuries they could afford. "They need you, Lord, the rich, the poor, and the clergymen of England who have forgotten you," he whispered.

As George walked the streets of London in his gown and cassock, many came out of their shops and houses to stare at him. One of the shopkeepers cried out, "There's a boy parson!" George quickly sent up a prayer, "You know how small I feel, Lord. Don't let them close their ears to your word because of my youth." His prayer was quickly answered.

Soldiers stationed at the Tower, and people from all parts of society came to hear him. Sunday after Sunday, as George preached at the Tower, he forgot everything but the people listening, and the message God was giving him for them. The joy of the good news of Jesus filled him and overflowed. Bible stories came alive as he told them. His voice was not like any the people had heard before. The chapel was full each Sunday. When his friend returned from school, George threw his arms about him and said, "God blessed me in spite of my fears, but I'm truly glad to go back to Oxford."

For the next eight weeks George held Bible studies, visited the charity schools and prison work of the Holy Club, and studied. Life at Oxford was good, but God had another plan for him.

For a second time George was asked to fill in as minister while a friend took classes. Not at the famous Tower of London this time, but a country parish of poor folks, mostly farmers. George was eager to help and was soon on his way to Dummer, a place that would change his life forever.

Barefoot children in clothes too big for some, and others with even the patches worn through crowded around him as he walked from cottage to cottage to visit the folks of Dummer. He was welcomed everywhere, given the best seat, usually a stool by the fire, and offered whatever the household had to share. Today, Monday, he meant to read to as many of the sick and old in his parish as he could. The children running ahead of him quickly shouted the news, "Minster's a-comin'." The first small thatched roof cottage he visited held a family of eleven. Inside, an old grandmother sat, as she did each day to look out for the youngest of eight children while their parents toiled in the fields. George had just entered the low door when the farmer and his wife and the rest of the children came rushing from the fields.

"Heard you was coming, Reverend," the farmer said, "we 'uns didn't want to miss a word you have to say." His clothes were old and not clean, but the man's eyes seemed to light up when George opened his Bible.

"You are welcome all of you. I plan to read the Word of God to grandmother here, and since the Bible is meant for all of us, I'm glad you've come to listen." George read them the story of the lost sheep and then explained it. While he spoke not a whisper of sound interrupted him, and when he rose to go there were tears in the grandmother's old eyes. George could hardly keep back his own, and as he turned toward the door the farmer too, and his wife, wiped their eyes.

"Can't none of us read a word, Reverend, and when we hear you read the Bible so plain, it's just like God writes it on our hearts, isn't it, Mother?" His wife nodded. The two escorted George a little way to the next house and as they left him to return to their work, he felt something he hadn't felt before. It was as much a privilege to preach to them as it was to preach to the great, the rich, the wise, the business people, anyone he had ever preached to before.

A letter had come to him in Dummer, from John Wesley begging for help in Georgia, one of the youngest colonies in America. John wrote, "George Whitefield, what if you are the man?" George wondered if God had sent him to learn from the poor in Dummer to prepare him for the mission field in Georgia, the poorest and newest of the colonies. It would be hard, he was young, and he would have to return to England in a year or two to Oxford for ordination as a priest in the Church of England. George walked along a country lane between fields of golden grain waiting to be harvested. He thought surely in America there were many who needed to hear the gospel. "I will gladly go if you send me, Lord." By the time his ministry at Dummer was over George was eager to go to Georgia.

Back at Oxford, Marcus was waiting for him. "I've sad news to tell you, George. Sir John Phelps has died. What will you do without the stipend he paid you to oversee the Holy Club and stay at Oxford?"

"I am sad at the loss of such a good man, but I will not need that stipend, Marcus. God will supply all our needs. And I shall certainly write and tell you how wonderfully he has when I'm in Georgia!" He chuckled at the look of surprise on his friend's face.

"You can't mean it. You are really going to Georgia?"

"Yes, and I can hardly wait. Charles Wesley is ill and must return home. John has asked me to come help him. I'm off first thing to apply to the church and government authorities in London for the necessary papers for mission work in the colony of Georgia."

"They will surely offer you a stipend as a minister to the parish in Georgia," Marcus said.

"Yes, and I will not accept it." Gently, George patted his friend's shoulder. "If God wants me in Georgia he will care for my needs in his own will and way."

The governor of the colony, General Oglethorpe, was in London on business and wished George to sail with him on his return to Georgia. The General hoped to finish his affairs soon. George planned to say goodbyes to his friends and family at Gloucester first, and then in Bristol.

His mother sat in Elizabeth's parlor and looked as if her heart would break. She did her best to change his mind "You are far more needed here in England," she pleaded. "I was so proud of you, George, and now you are running off to a savage land where no one knows you, and I may never see you again."

Elizabeth tried to comfort her. "George must do what God has called him to do. God will take care of him, and we will see him again when he returns for his ordination."

"I will still be here for the next few weeks," George said, "while I preach in the Reverend Harris's church at Stonehouse village." George did not know that it would be nearly a year before he left England, a year that would turn all England upside down.

Each week while he waited, George preached to large congregations that seemed to grow larger and larger as news of his preaching spread. General Oglethorpe was still unable to leave, and as invitations to preach came, George accepted them.

He was on his way to preach in Bristol. They were about a mile from the city when the coachman called down to him. "Looks like word has spread you're a-coming, Mr. Whitefield. I can't remember such a crowd excepting for the Queen passing through, and they're heading straight here."

George stuck his head out of the coach window and stared. People were on foot, others in coaches, some on horseback, and he could hear them now calling his name. Like a grand procession the people flocked around his coach escorting it into the city. George sat back inside the coach smiling at what he'd seen of the welcoming crowd. Like a small twisting vine, pride began to creep into his heart. He was famous! All those people knew who he was! All at once fear gripped his stomach and his face flushed with shame. "Forgive me, Lord. Wash me from the sin of pride," he cried. The honor these people were giving him belonged to God! George bowed his head. "They are hungry to hear your words, not mine," he said.

In Bristol church after church wanted him to preach. He spoke five times a week, and still the congregations grew larger and larger. People of all ranks of society and denominations flocked to hear him. Many came early to get into the church, and yet hundreds had to be turned away. Abel Dagge, the keeper of Bristol's Newgate prison had come early to hear Reverend Whitefield. He squeezed into the tightly packed pew and soon forgot the crowding as he listened to the message. Afterwards he found George and joyfully told him how God had touched his heart! From that day on Dagge was a changed man. He invited George to read prayers at the prison and teach every morning that George could come. The prison was famous for its filth and cruelty, but now Dagge was concerned for his prisoners. He did away with cruel practises and allowed no more abuse. He cleaned up the prison, and showed kindness to the prisoners. A famous writer imprisoned for his debts wrote of the kind treatment that had surprised him in Newgate.

George had hoped to sail soon for America, but once again the general was unable to leave. New invitations to preach kept coming, and George felt a powerful joy fill him—"This is what God planned for me to do all along."

The fame of his ministry in Bristol spread to London, and his slate calendar of preaching times quickly filled. Religious Societies that met at six in the morning asked George to speak to them. Not many often came at that early hour, but now so many made their way to church long before day with lanterns in their hands, that the dark streets looked as if they were filled with thousands of burning candles. For four months George preached, sometimes getting very little sleep, and preaching even ten times a week. People were leaving their lifeless churches to hear him, and their ministers were not pleased.

"Whitefield upsets all England," they said. "He sounds like a Puritan with his talk about sin and holy living. Such preaching has no place in the Church of England."

Among the nobility, Lady Huntingdon had only good to say of George, and invited many of her wealthy friends to hear him. One friend wrote to her, "It is monstrous to be told that one has a heart as sinful as common wretches, but I shall be most happy to accept your kind offer to accompany you to hear your favorite preacher."

George was visiting his friend James and as they talked George asked, "Have you heard that I am lately called a spiritual pickpocket? Some of the clergy say that their churches are empty, and I must be using a charm to catch people and their money."

James laughed. "I hear that they are calling for the Bishop to silence you. While others just wait for you to go off to Georgia, and hope you will never come back."

"I pray the Lord will open their eyes, James, and wake them all to himself."

I will win them with Guile

Word that George Whitefield was still in London brought thousands to hear him before he left for America. "His voice is like thunder straight to the heart, and 'tis the sweetest sound anyone ever heard," a shopkeeper told his customers. "The Bible comes alive," another added. "God has raised up this man for this hour, for England," others cried. George preached as often as he could, but the time to sail to America was close.

James had taken a holiday from the bookstore to help George. It had been a long day and the landlady had sent up some refreshments. As they both sat down to eat James said, "You are leaving behind hundreds of new believers in London alone. The need for Religious Societies where they can come together to study the Bible and pray is growing. The small Society I began is too full already, and we must begin another one."

George sat up straight. "And then another and another, James. I pray that Societies like yours will spring up all over England. Until the clergy begin to wake up and preach the truth, the Societies will be greatly needed. Our people must pray with us for men like you, James, to lead them."

Christmas came, George and James and a group of friends had spent the whole night praying! The following morning they went to church. The others had gone ahead, and as James and George walked together, George said, "After waiting for General Oglethorpe all this past year, it's hard to believe I'm to sail without him come the end of this Christmas week. I wish you were coming, James, but I'll write all the news as often as I can." George smiled at his friend. "I shall miss you, my brother."

"I will miss seeing you in my little bookstore looking through books and pointing out every treasure you find. But I will not miss all the buying you've had us all doing for the colony. All those books, clothes for the poor, cloth, thread, buttons, tin pots, penknives, shot, gunpowder, scissors, spoons, nails, axes, saws, shovels, and more, will finally be aboard ship. And we may all give thanks for that!" He laughed heartily.

"True, my supplies mount up," George said, "and there is still the baggage our little group of six will take. Our two teachers for the school we hope to start have more books, our two housekeepers have packed their pots and kettles, and James Habersham my assistant, has gathered enough quills, sealing wax, and stationery for a store."

At the end of the week George and those going with him boarded the ship. It was to sail within the next two days. George was in his cabin when a ship from Georgia arrived bearing John Wesley.

John had left the mission field in Georgia. The strict disciplined life he preached had failed to win over the people or the magistrates in the colony. No one wanted him to stay. When he heard that George Whitefield was already on board the ship to take him to Georgia, he did not know if he should try to stop him or let him go. When John wanted guidance from God he would cast lots. On a slip of folded paper he wrote the words, "let him return to London" and on another slip of paper "let him sail on to Georgia." Wesley closed his eyes and chose. The paper he chose said "let him return to London." Quickly John sent the message he was sure God had given him, with a note that George should not sail.

George read the note from John. His heart sank. "This casting of lots for guidance cannot be what God intends. I must try to see John before we leave port," he told the little group on board with him. But John had already left, and George returned to the ship and quickly wrote a letter to him. "I cannot turn back and desert my job as chaplain to the hundred soldiers aboard ship, or those others with me. And with you back in England the colony is without a shepherd. I must go, John. God will be with me there as he has been wherever he sends me."

George and his little group stood on deck as their ship, *The Whitaker* left the port, and soon all of England behind. Two other ships, *The Amy* and *The Lightfoot* traveled alongside *The Whitaker,* all of them headed first for Gibraltar to pick up more soldiers. The new soldiers, along with those already on board were needed to defend the colony of Georgia against the Spanish invasions from Florida.

As chaplain aboard ship, George decided to begin with public prayers the very next morning. No one came. Neither the soldiers nor the sailors, and not even the captain wanted a minister on board. None were friendly, and someone shouted loudly enough for him to hear, "Imposter, fake!" Instead of coming to the service, men gathered in little groups to play cards. Curses rose as they played. One man loudly used a handmade instrument not far from where George stood. George looked long and thoughtfully around him before he left.

Back in his room, he went quickly to his knees. "Lord Jesus, make me your servant, not just to these soldiers and sailors, but to the women and children and others aboard, and not just on this ship but I ask for all three ships in this convoy. Lord, help me to catch them with a holy guile!" When he rose from his knees he knew what he must do. He began by visiting the sick. Life on ship was hard and many were ill with fevers. George tended to them and used some of the medicines and nourishing foods he had brought with him. His sage tea and broth were welcomed. Evenings and mornings he read prayers as was the rule in the Church of England. Before a week was up he began a Bible class for soldiers. At first six men came and a week later the number increased to twenty. Slowly, George began to add preaching to the reading of prayers. But he was also finding his way into the lives of the officers, the surgeon, and the sailors.

He took breakfast with the gentlemen, gently letting a word or two for God enter the table talk, and sometimes it led to more discussion. He spoke to the surgeon who welcomed his interest. At night he walked on deck to talk to the chief mate and a sergeant. At eleven at night he sat down with the sailors in the steerage, and spoke with them, gently turning conversations to the things of God. It began to work and soon George was able to start a Bible class for the women on board while his assistant Habersham taught their children. Soldiers or sailors who wanted to learn to read and write were invited. Captain Whiting, the ship's Master, now gave George the use of his cabin for private prayer and study. Within a week the Captain asked George to read prayers and give a private sermon for himself and his officers.

It was not long before the gospel opened the Captain's heart to a deep concern for the soldiers on board. He ordered chairs to be put on deck with planks across them for benches so that everyone on board could come for services. *The Whitaker* became a floating chapel, including a male choir of soldiers who could sing. George's heart was full of praise to the Lord. However, it was soon to be tested when the calm seas turned ugly.

The morning began with a darkened sky and a wind that blew hard. By midnight a terrible storm broke upon the ship with gale force winds. By four in the morning the sea was a fearful sight as George went on deck. "Lord," he prayed, "protect us and all who are aboard this ship." He had never seen such an awful storm. The waves rose up mountain high and when they crashed upon the high quarterdeck he couldn't help whispering, "How great is your power, Lord!" With the next crashing wave he and his friend Habersham were forced to crawl on their knees to reach the people between decks who needed comforting. For a while the two sang Psalms and tried to calm the terrified people. Things fell and rolled around them as the ship rocked. The calmness George felt was from the Lord. But around him in the dim swaying lantern light children cried and many were seasick. The foul smells and heat between the decks made even George a little sick. When the storm was over and the ship finally reached Gibraltar, a military outpost known as the Rock, George was glad to go ashore along with the others.

At Gibraltar George was asked to preach. By the time the ship was ready to sail God had again done a mighty work. Crowds of a thousand filled the church, soldiers begged to sail on the Whitaker to be with him. Many came with gifts of food for the voyage. Back on board George visited the sailors as he had before, and now the men welcomed him gladly.

When the ships entered the trade winds and the sea was calm, all three ships drew close so that those on all the vessels could hear George preach.

Still not yet twenty-four, he stood to preach with the captains standing on either side of him. The beat of the drum called the soldiers to service, and to George the men in their red coats were like a forest aflame on the decks. God's gift of a mighty yet musical voice needed no more than the open sky and sea. Amazingly, when he preached his voice carried clearly to each of the vessels.

George and his helpers filled up the hours on board ship with ministry, but it was soon to be an even greater task. "Come quickly, Reverend Whitefield," the surgeon's boy cried. "There's fever below decks like we ain't seen afore. People are falling sick everywhere." George and Habersham followed the boy below. Already twenty or more folks lay moaning and burning up with fever. Day and night George tended the sick while the surgeon cared for new cases as the number of sick grew until at last there were no more new cases.

The final days on ship were filled with visits from soldiers and sailors who wanted to let George know what God had done in their lives on this trip. The sailor, who had called him an imposter that first day came to say, "I want to serve my Lord Jesus the rest of my life." George's heart was full of joy. The trip to America had taken four months by the time the Whitaker anchored off the coast of the colony of Georgia. They were about to step into the new world!

Savannah, Georgia was a clearing in the forest with about a hundred primitive cabins and a population of five hundred people. The southernmost settlement, a hundred miles away was a military outpost of roughly a hundred people. Between Savannah and Fredericka lay a handful of small villages. Counting those who had come with George less than a thousand people lived in Georgia. The first thing George did was to visit the Magistrates of the colony who received him kindly. He began services the next morning in the village town hall. It was also the church, with benches for the people, a gallery for the officials and a pulpit for the minister. Seventeen people attended. "It's a good beginning," George said.

James only smiled. George Whitefield would only preach to seventeen once. After that the town hall that only held a hundred would be packed and soon too small. James was right!

George was eager to visit all the settlements in the colony to help wherever he could. "Everywhere we go, James," he said, "the people's hearts are hungry for God's word." They were also poor and in need of the many supplies George had wisely brought with him. From Savannah to Frederica George carried out his plan to set up little schools for the children. "They are the hope of the future of Georgia," he said, "and must have a good education that includes the Bible and Christian living. In Georgia many of the people were debtors released from prison and transported to the colony for a new beginning. It was a harsh life for many of them who were poor and unskilled at farming. Some colonists were Swedish, some German. George gave out tools and supplies, purchased livestock for needy families, and even barrels of flour for a poor baker, and the good news of Jesus to all of them.

Three times a week George read to a houseful of people who could not read the Bible for themselves. He taught and preached, baptized children, and reached out with love and gentleness to the people. One farmer said, "Reverend Whitefield's the only man of God I ever heard talk so plain and easy with the likes of us." It was the same for servants, children, officials, young or old, transported prisoners, all who heard him found his messages plain and easy. They felt as if God meant the words truly for them. But for George, one heavy burden tugged at his heart: the terrible lives of the colony's orphan children.

Sadly, the number of orphan children in the colony was a growing problem. Life in Georgia, a frontier colony settled only three years ago, was hard and many parents died. Children left poor and orphaned were often abused, badly clothed, poorly fed, sometimes half-starved. Some were taken to work for a master or mistress who treated them as property and cared little for their welfare. When Governor General Oglethorpe a kind-hearted man, saw the terrible needs of the children and asked the new minister, Mr. Whitefield to establish an orphanage, George could hardly wait to begin.

When George came home and announced, "I have just been given the right to build an orphanage, thank the Lord, friends," those who had come with him cheered. No one was surprised. From the first days on the Whitaker, George had talked of the schools they would have for children. The terrible plight of orphans in the new world had gone straight to his heart!

George was young and strong and he knew how to plan! "With God's blessing this orphanage will become a refuge for children where they will find protection and care," he told the others. "We must do more than clothe and feed them; we will teach the Bible, educate them and help shape their characters."

On his way to the town hall, George stepped over muddy ruts in the path that was the main road. Here in the poorest colony, surrounded by wilderness and dangers there was no money to build decent roads, or to support an orphanage. He must take word of the needs of the colony and its orphans back to England where God's people could give to help the work in Georgia. Four months later the people who now loved him accompanied him as he took his leave.

George waved. When would he see them again or set foot in this place on the edges of the American frontier he had already come to love? He would take one more step before he returned to America. In England he would be ordained as a priest in the Church of England. George waved a final goodbye.

Thank God, the fields are open

The return trip to England on board *The Mary* began
with the winds against them. The storm grew so fierce
that hardened sailors feared for the ship. As seas rose
and winds raged tearing sails and splintering wood,
barrels and boxes of supplies went overboard. Only
small rations of food and water were left, too little to
satisfy anyone's thirst or hunger. George felt too weak
to walk about, but he was calm as he read his Bible
and prayed.

The strong winds drove *The Mary* turning her until
no one knew where they were. All hope seemed gone.
One of the passengers, a Captain Gladman, who had
been shipwrecked near Georgia and was returning to
England, could not understand George's peace.

"We are lost, and near death," the captain cried.
"Tell me, Mr. Whitefield, what is this hope of yours? I
confess I am terrified."

George grasped Gladman's hand as the boat listed
and drifted. "What you need, friend, is the good news
of Jesus. I have peace because I know His grace will
be all I need whatever happens." Gently and clearly
George spoke the gospel to the man. By the end of
the trip Gladman had become a Christian, ready to

serve the Lord Jesus, and had joined George's little group.

At last the lookout cried out "Land, land ahead." They had come to the coast of Ireland and the ship put into port safely. The next morning George and those with him set out to Dublin on horseback. When people heard that George Whitefield was there he was asked to preach at the Cathedral before leaving for England the next day. "You are not yet twenty-four years old," Captain Gladman said, "and already God has given you a ministry throughout England and in America. Your name is known in Ireland, and in Wales and Scotland too."

"God is indeed blessing his work," George said, "and I can only praise him."

They were soon back in England and George began his plan to raise money for the orphanage. "The trustees have given me a license to raise funds here in England for the building of an orphanage in Georgia, and I must visit the churches to tell them of the desperate needs of the orphans." George's plan quickly ran into trouble.

George and William Seward, a close friend and helper, had just come from another church closed to George. Like the others this minister also refused to let George talk about the needs of the orphans in Georgia. "How can the churches turn us away, William? Church law in the Church of England allows the use of its churches to raise funds for such charities!

They know that I have a license from the trustees to raise funds for the orphans."

William answered quickly. "These ministers just want you to stay away from their churches and congregations. They fear you now that you are back in England because their people listen to your message."

The following morning George read aloud the headlines from the official church newspaper. "Mr. Whitefield would do well to return to Georgia, and we shall do our best to see that he does so!" George put down the paper, and looked up at Marcus and William and Gladman seated around the breakfast table. "At least I am still welcome in four churches."

"Yes," Marcus agreed. "And you have been asked to preach twice each Sunday and five days of the week between." More preaching came as the people demanded they be allowed to hear George. In fifty-six days George preached fifty-seven times! The Religious Societies wanted him too, and by Christmas George was preaching and ministering to people from morning to midnight. "This is like nothing we've seen before," George said to the members of the Holy Club, "this is God's hand at work!"

Bishop Benson was ready to ordain George now as a priest in the Church of England. "I invite you all to come," George told his friends. Others came too, among them Lord and Lady Huntingdon. When the ceremony was over, it was time for him to preach his first sermon as an ordained priest of the Church of

England. In his hand George held the Bible, and when he began to speak a hush filled the crowded church. As George urged all who were there to see the love of the Lord Jesus for them, some could not help their tears. In the weeks that followed his preaching slate filled again and again.

The crowds who wanted to hear George were so dense people sometimes stood on stairs or on whatever place they could find. There was no noise once he began to speak. George always seemed to speak to each one personally. Once George saw a young boy with a lantern in his hand, perched on a ledge listening intently. When George lifted his hands to heaven, the boy lifted his too letting the lantern crash to the ground. George wondered later what had become of the boy.

Marcus was worried about how little rest George had. "I must preach wherever I can," George said. Often so many came that some had to listen through the windows. "There has never been a voice like this in England," people said. "Thousands are turning to God."

The enemies of George were asking, "How can we silence the voice of George Whitefield?" In spite of his opponents George was not silenced. People came, and the amazing voice God had given him could be heard for greater distances than anyone imagined possible. His enemies could weaken it only one way, turn the people against him! They would attack his words, his message, his trustworthiness, and his character! Attacks on his character came quickly.

A chaplain to the Prince of Wales accused George of teaching spiritual pride. "Mr. Whitefield speaks of a 'new birth', and tells the people they can know they are saved," he said. "This is spiritual pride," he declared. Next came an attack on George Whitefield's trustworthiness.

Marcus felt deep hurt and anger for his friend. "George, you need to do something. They say you stole the pulpit when you preached at St. Margaret's church last Sunday. The story is told that you waited while your friends locked away the minister who was to preach, and then arrived to take the pulpit yourself," he said. "How could they twist the truth so? We were late that night because the coach broke down," Marcus said. "It was a sexton who locked the minister's pew. And it was the church warden who came to say you were to preach and even led you to the pulpit."

"Sadly, such a story will do its work, and some will believe I will do anything to get into the churches to preach," George said. "Even steal the pulpit from another. One day the Lord will make all clear."

People still came to hear George, and the next Sunday he preached twice to a crowd of nearly a thousand. Hundreds more had to be turned away for lack of room. George was deep in thought that night. *"Could it be, Marcus, that I might preach without doors and walls, in the open air?"*

Marcus shook his head. "Now that would give your enemies something new to say. I think it is a mad notion, George." George had already exchanged letters with a preacher, Howell Harris, who preached outdoors in the hills and villages of Wales.

One morning George announced, "Friends, while I'm still here in England we must reach out to Kingswood and its coal miners. These people have no churches and no schools, and no clergymen go there."

Marcus knew the area. "Thousands live in Kingswood, colliers who work in the dark mines under terrible conditions. Their lives are full of danger, disease, and dirt," he said. "The place is despised and known for its viciousness, and Bristol folk fear them."

"Yes," George said, "but I long to tell them of Jesus' love." On the coldest February day in memory he and William dressed as warmly as they could and set out to call the people out of their pits and hovels to come to a meeting the following day. Two hundred people came. George stood on a small mound to preach. The message was not like anything they had heard. George's words spoke straight to their unchurched, unschooled hearts as he made the love of Jesus real to them. George saw the white streaks made by tears on the dirty faces of many of the hardened men and women touched by God's message. He promised to return the following Wednesday. A crowd of 2,000 waited for him. The final week 20,000 came, as farmers and townspeople and others stood by the side of the colliers they had once shunned.

"Lord, give me a voice like a trumpet," George prayed. "Give me eyes to see whatever you have sent me to use as a natural sounding board. Let the wind aid my voice, Lord, and give me wisdom to deal with those who might disturb these listeners." He had already asked the Lord for the message.

All throughout these months in England George had raised money for the orphanage. "We've collected two hundred pounds," he told his friends. "But before I go back to Georgia, I want to raise money for a school where there has never been one, a school here in England for the children of Kingswood." They cheered, and the money came. George appointed John Wesley to take over the work while he was in America.

Before he left Kingswood one of the colliers came to see George. "Sir," he said, "God sent you to us, Mr. Whitefield. We want you to lay the first stone for the new school. It will bless us to know your hand was the first on it." George laid the first stone and prayed for all who would one day enter the new school.

On the last night at Kingswood, as he and William were leaving, George turned to look back. "William, look at what God has done! Did you ever dream when you came to serve the Lord it would be so grand as this? When the churches are closed, He shows us another way." William had tears in his eyes and couldn't speak. George stretched out his arms. "These fields are our outdoor church and may hold as many as will come." He smiled broadly at William. "Now there is one more trip I must make, a quick one. Come with me to Wales, and we will meet Howell Harris together. He is the first traveling preacher to make the hills and fields of all South Wales his parish, and I hope to learn much from him."

When George saw Howell, a sturdily built man, though not tall, striding toward them, he cried out, "How much I have wanted to meet you!" Almost at once the three began a preaching tour. George soon learned from Howell how to use almost anything to stand on for a pulpit, a horse block in front of an inn, a table in the center of a street, or a stone wall. Howell preached in Welsh, and George followed with English. The week passed quickly. "We've slept little, prayed much, and loved every bit of serving the Lord," George said, as they parted.

Back in London there was still no sailing date, and George hoped to preach in Moorfields Park. It was a place where people came evenings and Sundays to see everything from bear baiting to dog fights. His friends warned him not to go. "You will never come out alive if you try to preach there," they said. George listened but knew he would go anyway. On the Sunday he chose, the word spread quickly, "Whitefield is coming." Great crowds waited for him and George felt a twinge of fear, but the people made way for him. He preached standing on a stone wall between the upper and lower Moorfields, and the people listened!

The Kensington Commons was another place George longed to reach. The commons, a twenty acre plot of ground held a permanent scaffold for hangings. Many of London's worst sorts, including pickpockets, came to watch the hangings, and the mob could get out of hand quickly. George prayed for the Lord's help. The crowd who gathered to listen to him grew to near 30,000. A hush rolled over them as George began. No one had spoken of God to them with such power before. George felt the words of God deeply as he preached to the people before him, and many came to the Lord that day. He returned to preach at Kensington and Moorfields to growing crowds. George spoke to them all of the love of Christ, the new birth, and the forgiveness of sins.

Now the time for George to leave for America was drawing close.

The Whole World is now
my Parish

The ship, *The Elizabeth* was ready to sail. George smiled as the young boy and two small girls, orphans he had rescued from the streets of London, stared wide-eyed at the great masts and sails above them. The boy of about ten, neatly dressed in clothes George had purchased for him, looked up at George. "Sir, I reckon she's the best ship in England."

George took his hand in his, "Yes, my boy, she's well built and will do splendidly to take us to America. The Lord Jesus who loves his children dearly will watch over us all the way. Now run along with Mrs. Dent who is waiting to settle you all in your cabin." Mrs. Dent was a widow who had come to mother orphans in the new world. These were her first charges. All of the group of eight men and four women going with George were leaving England with hearts ready to serve the Lord.

William and Captain Gladman stood at the rail watching the sailors work at the sails. "It's a sight I never tire of," the Captain said.

George came to stand by them. "Captain, you must miss commanding your own ship," he said.

Gladman was silent a moment, and when he spoke his eyes glistened. "Before I knew the Master, I could not have imagined doing anything else. Now, He is the Captain of my life and it will be a great joy to serve him."

George turned to face the Captain. "This new world needs to know him as we do," he said. "May he open the eyes of America to see him!" George was silent for a moment before he spoke again. "I am ready to go as an itinerant preacher to preach the good news throughout the colonies or in England, or wherever the Lord calls me."

"I think I know as much about sailing ships as any man, but I have not heard of an itinerant preacher before," the Captain said.

William spoke up quickly. "Am I right, George that an itinerant has no parish or church congregation of his own, but goes and serves many churches?"

"You come close," George said. "An itinerant preacher may preach in churches or outside of them, wherever he is led to go. While we are in America, the orphanage, Lord willing, will be our home base and from there we will make preaching tours through the colonies as the Lord leads. The world is now my parish."

Captain Gladman's eyes filled, as he said, "If God has called you to do this, he will bless this work even in America. I am ready to help anyway I can." The others said the same. It was late when they returned to the cabin.

For the next week George stayed in his cabin to pray and study his Bible. He'd been so busy preaching to others and defending himself from the opposition, that he had not seen his own faults, or needs. He thought of his failures and began to think he was not worthy to be a minister, not patient enough, not kind enough. Being well-known could so easily bring him pride, and the list went on. Day after day George told the Lord his fears, read his Bible and prayed. By the end of a week, peace filled his heart like an overflowing stream of fresh sweet water.

He wrote to Marcus, "I saw my sins so clearly this week that I felt I could not go on preaching, but the Lord showed me what I must pass on to you, dear brother." He thought a moment then wrote: "Satan will accuse us, but we may say with all our hearts, 'Jesus is my Righteousness.' He has called us, and he will keep us! Marcus, we need not fear! Our Jesus will let nothing pluck us out of His mighty hands. This is our support in all our trials!" As he sealed the letter it seemed to George as if the words he had just written were truly written on his own heart: Jesus is my Righteousness!

The rest of the voyage went quickly as George wrote letter after letter to encourage those who were spreading the gospel. To one he wrote, "Speak every time, my dear brother, as if it was your last. Talk to them, even till midnight, of the riches of Jesus."

The Elizabeth took eleven weeks to reach the eastern coast of America. They were in sight of land and white sea gulls swooped overhead on breezes that carried the smells of growing things. George stood next to the railing with William and the others, while the children pressed close to Mrs. Dent.

"There it is, children, America!" he said. "The colonies starting with Maine in the north to Georgia in the south, run down the eastern coast like a strip of ribbon 1300 miles long and mostly no wider than fifty miles. On one side of them is the Atlantic Ocean and on the other side is a vast wilderness where a great number of Indians live. Nearly a million people fill the colonies, and 150,000 of them are Negro slaves. We must pray God to help us tell them all the good news of Jesus."

Turning to William and Gladman, George said, "While our little family stays on board till Philadelphia, we will go on by land from Lewis Town. We can go by horseback to Philadelphia and get to know some of our new country. Philadelphia is the center of the colonies, and I plan to order wood and materials for the orphanage there. If God wills, I can preach the gospel and receive offerings for the Orphan House along the way." Both friends agreed heartily.

The Elizabeth stopped long enough for the three men to wave goodbye to the rest and go ashore. It was October 30, 1739. News traveled across the ocean by ship, and the colonies' newspapers were filled with stories of George Whitefield's great ministry in England's churches, and in the open air! Christians in the colonies were eager for his coming, and hoped that

Mr. Whitefield would help spread the good news of Jesus. The three men were soon on their way to Lewis Town, 150 miles from Philadelphia. In Lewis Town George was told, "Once you leave Lewis Town, you will be riding for miles through unsettled wilderness. You'd better hire a guide," their host warned them.

The guide William hired was a weathered-looking man who said little, but seemed to know his way. Soon there were no real roads. George marveled at the birds and wild animals they saw. Trees grew thick around them, some of which were new to George and his English friends. However, they had not seen a single person besides themselves, all day. It was ten at night before they came to a small, rustic tavern built in the middle of nowhere. They had ridden twenty-seven miles that day! The tavern keeper and his wife were plain, simple folk who offered what food they had, cider, eggs, and unleavened bread. To George it seemed like a feast. Fed and weary, George led them in a time of prayer and reading before bed. By eight the next morning they were on their way.

This time they rode nineteen miles before they reached a place to stop and eat. George invited their guide to sit near him, and in a short time the two were talking. By nightfall they had ridden fifty miles to an inn. The following day they rode sixty miles. Soon they were seeing large plantations and open country as they neared Philadelphia. It was eleven that night when they stopped at an inn in Philadelphia. George like the rest was weary and about to climb into bed, when a knock came at the door.

It was the guide. "Reverend Whitefield, I'll be on my way now, but there's something been eating at me since you preached in Lewis Town. I don't reckon, Sir, I'm a saved man, and I reckon it's time I did something about it. Could you help me?" George's heart leapt. Late into the night they spoke. And after tears and prayer the man left, thanking George and promising to look for him when George returned that way.

The following day William made final arrangements to rent a house for the family who would soon arrive on *The Elizabeth*. Philadelphia was a thriving colony with shops and goods to be had from its ship trade up and down the coast and with England. William, a wealthy man, had no trouble finding a fine large house. It was a joyful little troop that stepped onto land. The children were wide-eyed at all they saw. While the family settled in, George was asked to preach that evening at a Quaker meeting. Philadelphia was a city with many Quakers and churches of several other denominations. On the way William said, "Except for you, George, I know of no ministers of the Church of England who call Quakers their brothers in Christ."

George nodded. "If a man believes in Jesus Christ then he is my brother, Quaker, Baptist, Presbyterian, or Independent. It is my joy to preach in their churches, and wherever I may preach the good news of Jesus."

Whitefield is Coming!

The newspaper headlines read, "The city of Philadelphia welcomes the young Reverend Whitefield whose preaching has stirred all England!" On Sunday George preached to a full congregation at a Church of England church. Crowds came again on Tuesday, and by Thursday the people cried out for an open air meeting to allow the great numbers to hear. George agreed, and though it was a cold November evening, he stood on the Court House steps with his Bible held high before a sea of nearly 6,000 people. For the next three nights 8,000 stood outdoors to listen. On the last night he wrote in his journal:

> Before I came all was hushed, exceedingly quiet. The night was clear but not cold. Lights were in most of the windows all around us for a considerable distance. The people did not seem weary of standing, nor was I weary of speaking ... the Lord gave me strength ... My heart was filled with his love ... I thought I could have continued speaking all night.

He put away his journal, thankful there had been time to write in it. Most nights there was barely time to eat before people came to the house to hear more, and sometimes stayed far into the night.

George had been in Philadelphia for nine days preaching, when the clergy of the Church of England churches who welcomed him at first turned against his preaching. "George Whitefield will not call anyone a Christian who does not hold to the new birth he preaches," they said. One minister, who met George on the street, spoke for many of them when he said, "I am sorry to see you here, Sir."

George replied, *"And so is the Devil, Sir."* George was about to leave for New York, and added, "We go to New York tomorrow, but perhaps we shall meet again when we return to Philadelphia." Without a word the man strode away.

As George and William walked on, William said, "That gentleman will not be happy to see you again, but it's clear from the good Mr. Thomas Noble's last letter that you will be welcomed in New York. Mr. Noble has written begging us to stay at his house. And he has already put aside a good offering for the orphanage."

They were on their way to the shop of Benjamin Franklin the printer. Mr. Franklin had published two volumes of George's sermons and two of his Journals.

Though no one could know it yet, the name of Benjamin Franklin would one day become famous as one of the great Americans of his time. When Franklin first heard George preach he wrote, "The multitudes that attend his sermons are enormous ... He has a loud and clear voice, and ... may be heard and understood at a great distance, especially as his audiences, however numerous, observe the most exact silence." Franklin was amazed at the effect of Whitefield's preaching on people, and the changes that followed in the life of the town around him. "I cannot take the words Mr. Whitefield speaks into my own heart," he wrote, "but I do love hearing him preach. It is like listening to great music, truly remarkable."

Franklin, who was always curious, decided to find out how large a crowd could actually hear Whitefield preach. Franklin had been standing in an enormous crowd, and began walking backwards as far as he could still hear George. Then imagining his distance the radius of a semi-circle filled with listeners, allowing each two feet square, he computed that George could be heard by more than thirty thousand. The newspaper accounts of twenty-five thousand people in the fields listening to George were possible. "This young preacher is truly a good man, a gifted man," Franklin said. The two became lifelong friends.

In New York George went at once to the Commissary of the Church of England to ask for the use of the church. He never had the chance to ask. The Commissary strode from his office to meet George in the church hall. "I know who you are, and what trouble and division you are making, Sir, wherever you go!" he said. "You shall not use this church or any other under my authority. I bid you good day, Sir."

"I'll gladly preach in your fields, Lord, or anywhere you lead," George whispered as he left. That afternoon he spoke to hushed crowds in an open field, and that evening at a Presbyterian Church filled to overflowing. George preached wherever he could until time came for the return to Philadelphia.

The kindly Mr. Noble, their host, was sorry to see them go. "You are twenty-four years old, and God has already blessed you with a great gift. I hoped you could make a visit to the Reverend Jonathan Edwards in Northampton. He is the man God so greatly used to awaken people's hearts there, a true revival. They have heard of you, Reverend Whitefield, and pray that you may come and help them."

"I must go back to Philadelphia," George said, "but you are right that I need to go see Jonathan Edwards, and soon. I hope to learn much from that godly man."

On the ride back to Philadelphia George preached. Word spread that he was coming, and crowds arrived before he did. "How can so many come together in the middle of nowhere on such short notice?" he said to William. "It looks as though nearly a thousand have come on horseback."

When they returned to Philadelphia, only one Anglican Church was still open to George. The weather was bitterly cold, and he was glad to preach inside several times, but soon the large church became far too small. Once again the open fields became his pulpit.

George had purchased supplies for the Orphan House while William arranged a sloop, or sailing vessel, to transport the family to Georgia. Captain Gladman was eager to sail the sloop, while George and William and his secretary, Syms, rode horseback the 800 miles to Georgia. They would learn about the colonies and George would preach where he could. As they left Philadelphia two hundred horsemen rode with George and his friends to escort them for a while and wave them farewell.

Now there were no proper roads. In Maryland with its few towns and large plantations George found very little Bible knowledge. "They seem surprised that I speak to them about God and Christ," he said. At times between settlements they could not find even an inn to buy food for themselves or their horses. A planter sold them a little milk and ale, and a bit of provender for their horses, and an old woman gave them bread. George encouraged his friends, "Thank God for what he sees fit to give us, take heart and press on."

On December 10, a snowy, windy evening, they tried to cross the Potomac River into Virginia. They nearly lost both their lives and the horses. "We must turn back," Syms cried as his frantic horse lost its footing.

"We will go back," George shouted above the wind. "It's hopeless to try to cross this night." Wet and cold they turned the horses back and finally reached the ferryman's house. He had little to share with them, but the next morning they crossed the river safely. They still found no place to buy food. George wrote in his journal:

> *December 12: rode eighteen miles with little food, witnessed to a ferryman in Piscadaway, but could not find even bread or milk there.*

Late that day they reached a tavern and were given food and a bed in the kitchen. The kindly woman who owned the tavern kept her drinking patrons away from George and his small group that night.

In the colony of Virginia the commissary and the governor welcomed them kindly, and gave them food, and lodging. Along the way George wrote, "In North Carolina we have found scarcely any form of religion, and in South Carolina many of the ministers are like dry bones." Underneath their politeness, George thought the southern colonies seemed dead to God.

They traveled on bad roads, wet, swampy ground, and often saw no one for miles. At night they often slept in the woods listening to wolves nearby. Once when they were lost God sent an unexpected guide who led them to a small house for the night. And wherever they came to small towns George preached.

One night when lost in the woods William spotted a cabin and hurried towards it. As they drew nearer he beckoned to George and Syms to stay back. "They are Negroes and may be runaway slaves," he whispered coming alongside George's mount. "If the hunters are after them we mustn't be found here." George and Syms nodded and the three silently withdrew. After a twelve-mile ride they saw at last a great plantation and found shelter for the night. George asked to visit the slaves belonging to the house. Their cabins were windowless, hot, bare rooms. An old man was laying on the floor and several children sitting nearby. George spoke gently to the old man and told him of Jesus' love. The children listened eagerly. He did the same for the slaves who gathered to hear him outside the other cabins. That night George wrote in his journal:

> *These young Negro children are equal to any white children. My hope is to see a school of young Negroes singing the praises of Him who made them."*

Each time George visited the slave quarters on a plantation, he preached in words they could understand, that the Lord Jesus loved them, and the new birth was for them too.

Slavery was legal in all the southern states except Georgia. Only the Negroes seemed able to stand the heat as they worked in the fields. When the colony of Georgia called for the right to own slaves George believed there was a true need for their labor. He did not know that he would one day own a plantation to help fund the orphanage, and that every slave in the South would long to be on his plantation.

From the colony of South Carolina there were no roads at all, not even a trail to get them to Savannah,

Georgia. To reach Savannah they traveled by canoe, a two-day trip along the coast. When they arrived, Syms held up his slate. "Friends, we have been forty-three days since leaving Philadelphia. We have been in the Colonies for two months all told, and traveled from New York to Savanna," he said. He grinned, then added, "Before we left, I was told many times that only a handful of adventurers had ever made the journey we were about to begin, and certainly not a single preacher!"

A House of Mercy

George stepped back farther into the shade of a great oak on the edge of the new clearing for the orphanage. William had already moved back into the shade as they watched the men digging out stumps. "We're a good distance from town, and there's swamp land around us," George said, "but our grounds will be a safe place for the orphanage away from town and with plenty of room to grow. Can you picture it, William?" George pointed to the half-cleared land. "The main building will stand two stories high, with rooms upstairs for the children, staff rooms, and down below kitchen, offices, an infirmary and a school. Barns will be in back with the gardens."

William wiped his forehead. The day was hot and humid. "I'm sure it will be grand, truly," he said.

George leaned back against the tree. "It should be, and best of all it will be a place of refuge for children here in the poorest, most isolated of the colonies. The colony of Georgia is far too poor to support an orphanage. God has touched the hearts of many to give to the work, and I trust he will open the hearts of others like you, William. Your generous gifts have given us what was needed to begin building."

William shooed away a fly with his hat and said, "He is blessing his work everywhere you minister, George. Surely he will bless this place of Mercy. I'm pleased with the house we've rented in Savannah, just knowing that more than twenty orphans are sleeping well tonight, safe until we can move them here."

"Safe at last," George said. "I have never seen children so pitiable as the three young boys who came to us yesterday. Their masters put them to hard labor beyond their strength, and treated them worse than their animals. If all the money given for this work was spent in freeing just those children from slavery, it would be well used."

"Well said," Williams agreed, "It makes me sick to see children so thin and weak, filthy and lice infested, and their arms and legs black and blue from beatings. Who could mistreat them so brutally? The rags they wore had to be burned, and I don't think one of them has slept on a proper bed before."

"The youngest children remember little before they were orphans and placed out. Others come with memories of living on the streets, or in the poorest of homes," George said, "but here they will be loved and cared for." He opened his arms wide, "This will be a house of welcome for every orphan in Georgia. We will call it Bethesda, the House of Mercy."

"It's a fine name," William said, "and I say it cannot come too soon for the orphans of Georgia."

"Come with me to the village, William, and meet the widow who will teach our girls to spin and card. We can talk on the way." As they walked George laid out his plans. The children would go to school five hours of the day, and spend part of the day learning skills they could one day use to earn their living. "I have plans for more land, barns for cattle, a dock at the river front, and a ten mile long cart road from Savannah." George felt a flicker of pride as he said, "It will be the biggest road construction ever done in this colony, and the Trustees have agreed to help with the cost." William smiled as George began again to list things they needed.

The work was going well when word came that George's brother James, now Captain of a ship, had docked in Charleston, South Carolina. George left at once to meet him.

When George arrived, James was standing on deck and saw him come. "Ahoy, brother," he shouted. "come aboard."

The two embraced, and when George stepped back he studied his brother's face a moment. "You have the wholesome tanned look of a true sea captain, now," he said.

"It's the life for me, George, just as preaching is for you," James said. "You must tell me all about your work here, brother."

"I will, but first come tell me of your adventures and how the family does at home. I miss them all."

They visited long into the night, and said goodbye the following morning. Before he could leave Charleston, George was asked to preach. Afterward, many who knew of the orphanage work in Georgia gave money for it. George had never received so much for the orphanage before at one time. As he left many begged him to visit them when he next passed through Charleston.

By the end of March there were a hundred mouths to feed as the number of orphans grew larger. According to his license, George had the right to bring any orphan in the state of Georgia to the orphanage, and George did his job well, but his troubles were growing.

With a slow step and a heavy heart George came to speak to his gathered friends and staff in the meeting room at Bethesda. He had just returned from a long meeting with the Trustees of the colony, and must now tell them all what had happened. The room was quiet as George began. "The Trustees no longer approve of me as they once did," he said. "Since I have become an itinerant preacher, and not the minister in residence here they see me differently. I am now seen as outside the Church of England, and worse as someone who preaches in fields and fellowships with Dissenters, not a thing pleasing to them. Most grievous to them is that I do not hold to salvation by works, a thing that has greatly angered the Commissary over the Church of England in Charleston and others." George waited until his friends' comments died down before telling them the worst news. "The trustees have decided to place Bethesda under the rule of the local Magistrates."

Stunned by his words no one spoke except Mrs. Dent who simply said, "Oh my."

"There is more," George said. "All funds collected for the work are to be accounted for to the Magistrates. All expenses now and in the future are to be mine alone. And I am to pay a yearly rent for the orphanage. These things may be managed, but the rest of their demands go far deeper. The magistrates will now be the ones to choose which needy orphan children shall come to the orphanage. And sadly, they will also have power to remove children from Bethesda when they are old enough to go in to service." George waited as William and others protested, and then added, "There are to be no looms at the orphanage to teach spinning, and the Magistrates may visit and inspect when they like." The silence turned to more protests and groans over the things George had said were now in place.

George held up his hand, "I know how this news has seemed to change our plans for a house of mercy for all, a place to educate and nurture all the colony's orphans. The magistrates have no interest in such things, but I am determined we shall go on doing these things for every orphan God allows us to care for in his name." George led them in prayer, and ended with the plea, *"May this always be a place where those who come may find your love, Lord."* It was to be a constant struggle and a heavy financial burden for

George, but his love for the children, and the ministry at Bethesda would remain unchanged. They would be well educated, taught good skills to earn their living, and taught the Bible and Jesus' love for them. He was already planning to bring someone to Bethesda who would be a mother to the children and see to the good order of their home.

George was hoping for a letter from England that would bring him good news, but when it came his heart sank. He had written to his friends, the Delamots, back in England to ask for the hand of their daughter in marriage. It did not help his case that he had told them in his letter about the deaths of three of the women who staffed the orphanage. The Delamots refused. "We do not feel that Georgia is the right place for our daughter," they wrote. "It is still a frontier with all its hardships, including the terrible heat of summer, Indians, and threats from the Spanish." George felt this new loss keenly, but put it aside as he prepared to leave on a spring preaching tour to New York and Philadelphia. His plan for the tour was to preach once in each place and then once again on the return trip. Spring was the best time to head north. The night before the journey, he slept little and prayed much. "Lord, you have called me to preach your truth here in America, but I cannot do it without your help." In the morning George, Syms, and William boarded the sloop for the first part of the journey.

Their boat arrived in the colony of Delaware, and word ran from place to place that Mr. Whitefield had come. People left what they were doing and hurried to hear him. That morning as George preached with all his heart to a large crowd, many wept. People had come far to hear him, and George agreed to speak again that afternoon.

The air was warm and the sky above a brilliant blue as George arrived at the open field where people already waited for him. He stood on a wooden platform and was about to speak when the sound of thundering hoof beats filled the air and clouds of dust rose in the distance. George watched as the horses and their riders drew nearer. The lone rider who led them motioned the others to stop, and slowly walked his horse close to George's platform. "Reverend Tennent," George cried out. It was an old friend, an elderly Presbyterian minister George knew from an earlier visit.

"Yes," the old man shouted, "and behind me are two hundred of my congregation come to hear you. So give us time to settle our horses so we can hear what the Lord has given you to tell us this day." George waited smiling right down to his heart to see his friend and so many others with him.

The following morning George and his friends arrived at their next stop to find nearly three thousand waiting for them. There was little time even to eat. George was eager now to reach Philadelphia. "I am longing," he said, "to see how it is with those who came to the Lord on our last visit there. We must press on."

A Bold Itinerant Preacher

When they reached Philadelphia, George went first to the Church of England church to ask to speak there. He was quickly refused by the commissary in charge who had heard of George's bold preaching of new birth, and how the people followed him.

"Well, Syms, that did not take long," George said, as the two of them left the church. "But God will supply us a pulpit." At the age of twenty-five, he was the best known preacher in England and now in America, thousands came to hear the young Reverend Whitefield. The people of Philadelphia wanted George to preach indoors at least during the winter, and soon built a large wooden building for his use. Converted ministers of any denomination were to use it too.

"Perhaps," Benjamin Franklin suggested, "we ought to allow Mohammedans or anyone of any religion to use the building." George gently insisted that only evangelical preachers use it. Franklin finally agreed, and the new building became a public house of worship on Sundays and a charity school for children the rest of the week. Soon the school became an Academy, and then a College, and later the University of Pennsylvania.

William put down the paper he had been reading as George entered their lodging. "You are just in time, George, to see your letter to the slave owners of the South. The newspaper reports that they are furious with you for saying that most of them treat their slaves worse than brutes, work them as hard as the horses they ride on, and take better care of their animals than their slaves. You call them monsters of barbarity, and say, if slaves should ever get the upper hand, the judgment would be just." William ran his hand down the page. "Ah, here you say I have seen your plantations, your spacious homes, sumptuous fare. And my blood runs cold when I think how many of your slaves have neither good food to eat, nor proper clothing to put on, though most of the comforts you enjoy are from their labors. And here, George, you use the Bible to warn them." William read aloud, "'Go to now, ye rich men, weep and howl, for your miseries that shall come upon you. Behold the provision of the poor Negroes, which have reaped down your fields, which is by you denied them. Their cries have come into the ears of the Lord of Sabaoth!'"

George put down the saucer of coffee he had picked up. "I used the word Negroes where the Bible says laborers. I do not know if buying a slave is a sin, but I know the way the slaves here are treated is sin. How often a poor Negro has come to me and asked 'Do I have a soul?' My heart breaks as I tell them they have a soul, and it is precious to the Lord Jesus. You know that when

I preach, I speak to the black man as well as to the white, and freely offer Jesus to them both."

William laid aside the paper. "God has gifted you to reach out to black and white, rich and poor with his word in ways that all may understand. I have heard of one Negro who repeats your sermon word for word from memory to others."

George nodded. "I pray that one day we can build a school for Negroes here in Philadelphia."

William smiled broadly. "Good, George. Captain Gladman and I will do our part back in England to raise support for such a school. And when we return we hope to bring people and supplies for Bethesda. You have my bill of credit here and may draw upon it for what funds you need."

Before the week was out William and Gladman sailed for England. George did not know that he would not see William again on earth. When the news came of William's sudden death, he mourned the loss of his friend and helper. William had given much to the ministry.

"Ah, Syms," George said, "he was a true servant of the Lord Jesus, and we shall miss that good man." George covered his face with his hands for a moment. "Sadly, he did not leave a will. We shall have to pay back the bill of credit we drew on, and there will be no more, but God will supply our needs. Our work at the orphanage will go on, but we must leave the school for Negroes to another to build."

The following day George and his companions rode for seven hours. A gathering of five thousand was waiting for them. As George dismounted he stumbled. Syms and one of the men quickly steadied him. "You are pale and trembling," Syms said.

George's body felt heavy and his legs weak. "It's been a long day." They had ridden in heat with little rest or food. When they had eaten, George went immediately to the crowds waiting for him. He wanted to preach but could he? He prayed and as he began God strengthened him. He forgot his tiredness, his powerful voice was back, and he was filled with the words of the message. George wrote in his journal that as they traveled on to New York this happened more times. When he had been so weak for want of sleep and the hard journey he thought he might not be able to preach, but God had strengthened him. "With God's help," he said as they traveled on, "we will finish this preaching tour." Thousands gathered to hear him along the return journey to Philadelphia; God was blessing the work. George was surprised when an old enemy appeared.

George was preaching in a small town when a woman in the crowd threw up her hands and began wailing loudly. Soon she fell to the ground rolling and twisting in a fit. Another woman, and then two men did the same. The fits lasted sometimes for more than a day. "The tears that come to a broken heart before God, are not like this, nor the joy of a thankful heart that turns to the Lord Jesus. These wild behaviors come from Satan's wildfire that he sows among us," George said. "As long as the work of God is going on, the devil will try to bring an evil report on it." George gathered those who were with him to pray and ask the Lord to rebuke the devil. "We must teach our people that this behavior is not from God," he said. When it happened another time George quickly gathered his people to pray. After that the wild fire disappeared and did not come back again to his ministry.

The summer heat was already fierce. George was weary from the miles of travel, and the heavy load of preaching and ministering day and night. He had preached throughout Charleston though it was the month of July and hot. The Commissary of the Church of England in Charleston had publicly condemned George for preaching the "new birth," and ordered him not to preach in any public church in the province. He warned George that if he did so, then by his authority as Commissary he would suspend George.

George continued to preach in open fields, in meeting houses, and in Dissenters' churches where Baptists and others welcomed him. The Commissary was outraged. The Commissary of Charleston now declared George suspended. "We decree and declare that the said George Whitefield, for his excesses and faults ought to be corrected and punished ... we do suspend him from his office." The Church of England ministers who wanted to be rid of George Whitefield, could now say he was defrocked, an outcast from the Church of England. The people should no longer listen to him.

"I am a resident of Georgia and you have no authority to suspend me," George said. George paid no attention to the decree. On the ride back to Savannah he preached many times. They reached Bethesda in the terrible August heat of a Georgia summer.

"This climate is bad for man and beast," Syms said. "Every day I see it draining your strength, George. You need to leave here and go north, up to Boston and Northampton."

George had little appetite or energy, and longed for even a little relief from the heat. "A visit to Reverend Edwards in Northampton might well refresh our spirits too," he said. They left by boat in mid-August for a fall tour that would take them to New England, then back to New York, Philadelphia, and Charleston. When they landed in the colony of Rhode Island, George said, "I feel relief from the heat already, and my strength is returning, praise the Lord!" That afternoon he preached to three thousand people.

In Boston George preached again and again to great numbers. On the Boston Common 23,000, the largest crowd ever known in America up to this time came to hear George. "We need to pray God will raise faithful laborers to carry on this work," George said. At Harvard College he spoke before the students. His powerful cry that without new birth in Jesus all were lost struck the hearts of people and turned them to Jesus. Many wept including the students. Harvard's leaders and professors were angry he had preached about new birth in their school. George wrote a letter gently apologizing for any wrong these men felt he had done them, and encouraged them to see what the Bible said about the things he preached.

In Northampton, Jonathan Edwards was waiting for them. Edwards was a tall man, taller than George who was also above average in height, but to George he seemed a spiritual giant. Edwards wrote later of their visit, "... the congregation was extraordinarily melted by each sermon Whitefield preached." Edwards too had wept.

Mrs. Edwards wrote to her brother about Mr. Whitefield, and said, "He is a ... devout and godly man ... he speaks from a heart aglow with love ... a born orator ... his deep-toned yet clear and melodious voice ... is perfect music."

George left the Edwards' home feeling deeply touched by this happy, godly family. Syms had slowed his horse to wait for George, and as George caught up with him, he said, "Syms, I think it is time I had a godly wife."

"Well, sir, it shall have to wait for now," Syms said, and grinned.

As they rode towards Savannah it was clear that God was blessing the work George had begun there. Many came to tell him how their lives had changed. One man saw George and ran to embrace him in a bear hug. "Reverend Whitefield," he said, "I once paid any sailor on an incoming boat if he could tell me a swear word I didn't already know. Now, Sir, thanks to your coming, I live to tell the good news of Jesus." His tears of joy were real, and so were George's.

Letters waited for George in Savannah. One of them caused him to gasp. "Syms," he said, "I must return to England. John Wesley has published a sermon on Free Grace, saying that God does not elect those he brings to himself, we choose him and become Christians." George shook his head. "No man could ever choose God if God did not first choose him. John is saying that what I teach is a doctrine of the Devil. He cannot see that faith and repentance are God's gifts to us." George handed the letter to Syms. "Marcus writes that many of the people we left in John's care now follow John's teaching and others long for me to come and help them."

Syms shook his head. "What you teach is from the Bible not the Devil. You must go back and show them." By Christmas, George, Syms and James, a friend and helper, were ready to leave for England. Their ship, *The Minerva,* sailed on January 24. As the men stood at the rail watching the coast of America grow smaller, George said, "We found so many people in this new world, hungry to hear God's truth, I long to stay but first I must go back to England and answer John's accusations."

George turned away to gaze out to the open sea before them. "While we are in England I must also raise money for the orphanage. I now owe 1,250 pounds for the orphan house, and am threatened with imprisonment for debt."

You Must Cover Your Ears

The Minerva docked safely and George and his companions stepped onto England's shore. It was March, 1741 and George had been away from England for over a year. Marcus was waiting for him. George greeted him warmly, but Marcus was not his usual cheerful self and at once began to tell George of the troubles waiting for him. "You will find things much changed," Marcus said. "Even in Moorfields some of the people believe that you are teaching wrong beliefs. John stood before them one night and tore the letter you wrote in your defense into shreds." Marcus swallowed hard and went on, "He has forbidden them to listen to you, George. He warns them to cover their ears when they pass you preaching in the fields."

George bowed his head. When he looked up he said, "Then we must begin to minister to our people again." George was soon back preaching in the fields. At first the crowds who had not left to follow the Wesleys were small. God had given George a voice that carried powerfully, clearly, winningly, and others began to stop and listen. Many of those who had left returned. Now the people wanted a shelter where they could listen to George out of the cold and rain, and built a large wooden building. "Sadly, I fear it is a bit too close to the Foundry where John is preaching," George said, "but it may be temporary. We'll call it The Tabernacle." Marcus, once again cheerful, smiled. Next they built a society-room at the Tabernacle with a school, a place to help the poor, and a workshop to employ some of them. After five weeks George was ready to go to Bristol and Gloucester."

In Gloucester people were eager to hear him. As George preached it was clear to all that he did not teach the devil's doctrine, but the Bible's truth. In Bristol the people who now followed John came to tell George of a new belief John was teaching that one could be perfectly sinless. George listened carefully to those who said they no longer sinned at all. When one woman said "I have been perfect for twelve months," George asked her if she had ever prayed for pardon for sins and she replied, "No, I have not committed any sin." A gentleman told George, "For three months past, I have not sinned in thought, word, or deed. I am free from in-dwelling sin, and I believe it is impossible for me to sin." George shook his head as he told these stories to Marcus and Syms. "They deceive themselves," he said. "How often I have prayed for forgiveness of sin, and each time our Lord Jesus in his deep love and kindness has forgiven me."

Marcus nodded, "It's the same for me, and the rest of us I'm sure," he said.

George held up his Bible. "This is the truth we teach, and pray God to make clear. We need to pray that God will heal the differences between John and us in time." God did answer his prayer and healed their friendship. John no longer accused George of teaching the Devil's doctrine, and though they didn't agree on minor differences they agreed that the gospel must be preached to all people. When he could, George often helped with the work in John's Societies, even enduring bed bugs on one trip.

Syms was sorting mail and George had just read one from Scotland. "Syms, it's from Pastor Erskine of the Associate Presbytery in Scotland. Their churches are no longer part of the National Presbyterian Church of Scotland, and they would like me to come and preach. Since I've already planned a trip to Wales, I will take the invitation and go first to Scotland."

George landed in Scotland and did not see any from the Presbytery waiting for him. Instead he was welcomed by a group of evangelical ministers who had not left the National Presbyterian Church of Scotland, but preached the good news of Jesus in their churches. "Come preach to us," they begged. George promised he would, but first he needed to speak to the men of the Associate Presbytery who had invited him to Scotland.

The meeting did not go well. The men of the Associate Presbytery had their own church government and rules. They insisted George must preach only in their churches. When George asked why, they answered, "Because we are the Lord's people." George would also have to accept all of the Presbytery's rules and ways, and they promised to help him see how right they were.

George was deeply saddened. "I cannot join you then. I have no interest in your church governing or rules, and I cannot preach only to your people. I am an itinerant preacher and must preach the gospel to all wherever the Lord leads me." George left and the men of the Presbytery closed their doors to him.

George went to Edinburgh to preach. Many wanted to hear this famous young preacher and the crowds were large. In a note to Marcus he wrote,

> Over three hundred people have come to the Lord Jesus here in Edinburgh. I am ready to leave here and preach as far as I can around the city for the rest of my time here in Scotland.

He continued preaching for three months more. His messages blazed with God's fire, and people turned to the Lord in churches, in parks, at old people's homes, in the slums, and in private houses.

At one meeting place George greeted a Quaker, a stout man wearing the tall black Quaker hat. As always George wore his black wool preaching robe. The man held out his hand and said, "Friend, George, I am as thou art. I am for bringing all to the life and power of the everlasting God. Therefore, if thou wilt not quarrel with me about my hat, I will not quarrel with thee about thy gown."

"*Friend,*" George shook the man's hand heartily. "*I wish all of every denomination were thus minded.*"

On his way to preach in Aberdeen, George and a companion stopped at the house of a poor widow in desperate need. When they entered the bare cottage George saw several children huddled near their mother. The poor widow looked worn and frail. The children's faces were thin and pale, their clothes small protection against the cold. His heart was touched, and quickly George searched his pockets and gave five guineas to the widow. After they left, it was not long before his traveling companion said, "How could you afford to give her such a sum?"

George answered, "God brought her need before us so that we could help."

They had ridden a good way more when suddenly a highwayman rode out from behind a clump of trees, and demanded their money. They gave him all they had, and the robber fled away. George turned to his friend and said, "How much better it was for the poor widow to have the five guineas than that thief." They rode on thankful to be unharmed, but scarcely any time passed before the highwayman was back. This time he demanded George's wool coat. George gave him the coat. With a loud guffaw, the robber tossed his own thin ragged coat to George. "It is better than none," George said as he put it on.

Glad to see the last of their highwayman, George said, "Since he has taken my coat and all the money we

had between us, I do not think we will see him again."
When they saw the man returning again, George
cried out "This time we must out race him to the next
village, or I fear for our lives."

George and his companion rode at a gallop with
the sound of the robber's horse far too close behind
them. To their joy as they neared cottages they saw
help already coming. The man was caught, and after the
excitement had calmed George took off the robber's
ragged coat, feeling as he did so a small bundle inside
the pocket and drew it out. George's laughter rang
out in the cottage as he opened the packet and found
one hundred guineas. When he could finally stop he
said, "The Lord has given me far more than I gave the
widow. It is no wonder the fellow was after me. This
gift will fill many a need, and what a story we shall
have to tell."

George often spoke about the orphanage. By the time
he left for Wales, the Scottish people had given enough
for the orphanage to pay all he owed but 200 pounds!

Among those who heard George and became a
friend was Lord Leven, his Majesty's Commissioner
to the General Assembly of the Church of Scotland.
When George announced that he must go on to visit
Wales, Lord Leven insisted, "Well then, you must take
one of my horses for the journey." The horse was a
fine animal, but it was not the horse that set George
to singing as he left for Wales. He was on his way to
Wales to get married to the widow Elizabeth James

who lived in Abergavenny. His friend Harris Howell had said of her, "In Abergavenny there is a good woman that if I were a marrying man I would marry her. She is a woman of strength of character, good sense, and she is devoted to the Lord. She would be a good wife for you, George, a gift from God." When George had been in Wales earlier he had met with her and found himself deeply attracted to her.

Elizabeth James was small and plain, but she was a woman whose faith showed in her quiet confident manner. They had written to each other, the widow had finally agreed to marry George.

The marriage took place at Caerphilly, and Howell was best man. The couple spent a week at the cottage in Abergavenny. Both knew that not even marriage must stand in the way of George's ministry. "One day, my dear, I hope we will work together at the orphanage, but now I must return to London and Bristol. All too soon it was time for George to leave. I will find lodgings for us in London as soon as possible," George promised. Elizabeth stood at the cottage door to watch as he rode away. George was back for Christmas, but left again soon after. It was three months before Elizabeth could join him in lodgings in London.

At last Elizabeth was becoming used to George's habits of rising at four in the morning. He was never late, he was neat and clean, and very self disciplined, and he loved a simple meal of pig knuckles. He was also meek and quick to sacrifice himself for others.

"Elizabeth, you are such a help to me," George said. She had just copied a pile of letters he'd asked for.

"And you, dear husband, to me," Elizabeth said. "I have grown so much in the things of the Lord. I loved the book you gave me to read last week, and I am so grateful for a husband that wants me to learn all I can."

"At least this winter I am to preach indoors at The Tabernacle, and you shall see too much of me I fear," George said.

"That, my dear, can never be. It will comfort me come spring and you are gone to the fields to preach," she said. Elizabeth was a devoted wife, and George a concerned, gracious husband. "I know that God is using you to awaken people to himself all over England, Scotland, Wales, and America," Elizabeth said. The opposition to his ministry saddened her. In a letter to a friend in Wales she wrote,

> *My dear husband is ridiculed in plays, denounced for his powerful preaching, refused pulpits in the Church of England, and preached against in dead churches. He longs for them all to hear God's message ...*

When George returned from preaching in an amusement park with mud and stains on his robe, Elizabeth patiently cleaned them. This day someone had thrown rotten eggs. "My dear," he said, "the merrymakers who threw those eggs quieted down soon after. I have no doubt some of them went away with the Lord's word ringing in their ears."

Elizabeth looked up, her dark eyes bright. "All over England and America God is bringing a great awakening. Those who do not want such a thing will do their worst."

"God has blessed his word and brought many to himself today. For such blessing I would willingly give my life," George replied.

A Great Joy and a Deep Sorrow

On a May morning, under blue skies with white seagulls circling above their boat, George and Elizabeth sailed for Scotland. George breathed deeply as they watched the shores of England grow smaller. "A sea journey is better than any medicine I know, Elizabeth."

"Yes, my dear husband, and you have needed this for a long while," she said.

George took a deep breath of the sea air. "It will be good for both of us. When I think of the hundreds of people turning back to God through the work going on in Scotland at Cambuslang, I feel it is a great privilege to be asked to help." Elizabeth smiled, pleased to be going with George to Scotland.

"I did not get to Cambuslang though I was near it on my last trip to Glasgow. The Reverend McCulloch in Cambuslang started teaching about new birth in Jesus, and people began coming and have not stopped. Workers are much needed." George placed an arm about Elizabeth's shoulder. "Pray, Elizabeth, that God will touch every corner in Scotland." A week later they landed in Edinburgh.

The city turned out to welcome them. When they left for Glasgow, a crowd of 20,000 was waiting. God blessed the message everywhere George spoke. One night, after a late meal George turned to Elizabeth and said, "I must write a letter to the men of the Presbytery who first invited me to Scotland, and now denounce me to their people. I must try to make peace with them."

Elizabeth's eyes filled with tears. "It is not in you to hold anything but forgiveness for others." Elizabeth wrote as George dictated a letter to the men of the Associate Presbytery begging them not to let small differences cut them off from each other. He signed it, "Your younger brother and servant in the Gospel of Christ. G. W." Elizabeth sealed it ready for delivery. There was no response.

It was July when George entered Cambuslang. The crowds that gathered in the open air were enormous! As many as three times in ten hours he preached to them. "I have never seen anything like this even in America," George said to Reverend McCulloch. People stayed on far into the night. In the fields all around them George could hear prayers and praises, some until daybreak.

The following Saturday and Sunday crowds of 20,000 came to the large natural amphitheater near the church, a great grassy place bordering on a ravine. Tents to shelter the speakers who had come to help were put up, one at each end, and another in a nearby field. No one had ever seen such a sight in Scotland before! George wrote of it to Marcus, "It is like the

Bible story of the Passover in Josiah's time. I preached under the shelter of one tent, while another spoke in the other tent. Hundreds have come to faith in the Lord Jesus, and many have awakened to God! I have been asked to return in a month's time." When he did return the crowds in Cambuslang had swelled to over 30,000 people.

The Associate Presbytery, angry that they had ever asked George to come to Scotland, now attacked the revival at Cambuslang. "George Whitefield and the others are frightening the people into frenzy. This is a work of the Devil," they declared. "George Whitefield is an idolater from the anti-Christian field of England." It was true that some people wept, and some groaned as they listened, and those who came to Jesus were joyful, but there was no wild fire here. As George read their angry letter to the public it was the last item that made him sigh deeply. "George Whitefield has come to Scotland to gain money for himself by using the needs of the orphanage in Georgia as a cover up."

George was silent, and when Elizabeth asked if he would write another letter to these men, he said, "Those dear men, I pity them. Writing again to them, I fear will be in vain." Elizabeth knew he had already forgiven them.

News of George's ministry in Scotland soon reached the American colonies and George's old enemies at once sent word that he was not to be trusted. The pamphlet from America accused Mr. Whitefield of being a fanatic who encouraged people to outbursts of uncontrolled behavior, and also accused him of collecting money for the orphanage and keeping it for himself. "I am already accused of this here in Scotland by our opponents." George looked away from the written accusations. "How the world is mistaken about my circumstances: worth nothing myself, and yet looked upon to flow in riches!" he said. "This time I must write a clear defense for the sake of Scotland and for the Colonies."

"You are no thief, George, and I cannot tell you how glad I am that you will clear your name," Elizabeth said. George published his defense with a full financial accounting of the work at the orphanage.

George was preaching in Edinburgh when a letter came from John Wesley. "It is so good to hear him call you brother," Elizabeth said.

"Yes, and John says though we still have some differences they will not keep us from spreading the gospel as brothers. He writes to tell of terrible persecutions he and his people are suffering," George sighed. "We must pray for them and encourage them." As Elizabeth took the letter, she thought of the terrible times of persecution she had seen in Wales as their friend Howell Harris preached the gospel. She too had been chased by unbelievers in her home village in Wales.

Back in London Elizabeth settled down in their lodgings while George preached. These days Elizabeth smiled often. She and George were going to have a baby!

George, whose heart went out to every small child they met, was to have a child of his own! "I will do my best, Elizabeth to see to your care while I'm gone, and I'll return as often as I can." On his next return George said, "You need a ride in the fresh air, Elizabeth. Let me take you for an airing in the chaise. It will be good for you." The air was cool and crisp and George was enjoying the outing when a gray flash of something small ran in front of the horse making him swerve wildly. "Hold on, Elizabeth," George cried. Elizabeth grabbed hold and seconds later the chaise overturned and landed in the ditch. Elizabeth was thrown across George who lay sprawled in the mud. Slowly Elizabeth managed to roll off George and sit up. As George got to his knees, and reached to help her, his anxious look and mud spattered face struck Elizabeth funny. She laughed and said, "This was good for me?" Except for a few bruises and a lot of mud, neither were hurt. "No more exercise for you," George said, "I promise." When the time came to leave again, George promised to hurry back. Elizabeth and her nurse companion waved him goodbye.

It was October and George had preached from a balcony to thousands below in the street. He was thinking of Elizabeth and writing a letter that evening when a knock came at his door. He supposed it might be someone with questions. Instead it was a messenger with news that Elizabeth had borne a son!

Thanking the Lord, George left everything, and hurried to London eager to see Elizabeth and their son. At the house they were renting, George ran up the stairs and into the bedroom. Elizabeth smiled at him from her bed, and offered him the tiny bundle that was his firstborn son. George could not keep back the tears of joy that ran down his face, as he cradled the little one in his arms. "My dearest wife, I feel a strong impression, a feeling I am sure is from God, that our son will grow up to be a preacher. What do you think of the name John?"

A few days later, standing before a hushed congregation of thousands, George held his son high. "His name is John, and he will be a preacher." Afterward many said that surely this little one would follow in his father's footsteps just as George had said.

By January George could no longer afford rent money for their lodging in London. Elizabeth looked up from baby John nested in her arms. "Dear husband, you must not mind. We shall be fine. My cottage in Wales will be a good home for our little son. You will come as often as you can. And when we are able to afford lodgings here in London again, we shall come back."

"I will long for that day," George said, "and until then I will come as often as I can to see you both in Wales." George paced the room before he stood and said. "The weather is cold and the journey by coach will be long, Elizabeth. You must take Mrs. Jennings the nursemaid with you. You will have to stop halfway on the trip and stay with my brother Richard and his wife at the Bell Inn. It's a good inn and you and baby

John can rest there for several days before you go on to Wales. I'll come as soon as I can."

Elizabeth and the baby and Mrs. Jennings had gone as planned. George finally finished his work and was on his way to Gloucester. He arrived at the Bell Inn at last, anxious to see Elizabeth and little John. In his eagerness, George did not notice the black draping at the front door. But his older brother Richard with tears streaming down his face met him at the door. Before he could say a word, George knew at once something was wrong. "Is it Elizabeth?" George whispered. "Is she well?"

"Yes, Elizabeth is well, but oh George I fear your little son is gone. He became sick shortly after they arrived here, and the doctor did all he could, but it was not to be."

George could barely speak, but as he went up the stairs to kneel by Elizabeth he whispered, "The Lord giveth, and the Lord taketh, blessed be the Lord." How many tears he and Elizabeth shed together, George could not have told. By the time of little John's funeral He felt God's strengthening holding him up. Kneeling down with Elizabeth, they prayed together, wept together and laid their tiny son in the church where George preached his first sermon, the church he had been baptized in. "It is well with our child," George said through his tears.

"Yes, I know," Elizabeth whispered, barely able to speak. "All things work together for good to them that love God. He was a gift," she sobbed, "and I will miss him as long as I live." After the funeral Elizabeth wanted to leave for Wales as soon as she could. "I will be with friends in Abergavenny," she comforted George.

Two days later, he and his brother Richard watched the coach leave with Elizabeth back to Wales. "I have learned a hard lesson, Richard. Four months ago I stood in front of the people of Gloucester and announced that our newborn son would be a preacher. I had such a strong feeling he would be a preacher that I was certain it was from God. I was wrong, Richard. We must not mistake such feelings as our guides."

Richard laid his hand on George's shoulder. "You are right, brother. It may turn out to be a feeling that is not from God. With all my heart I wish the child had lived. But now you have a ministry waiting for you to call many to new life in the Lord Jesus." George embraced his brother and with a final farewell boarded the coach to London.

There were now many Societies of true believers who were called Methodists for their faith in the Lord Jesus. And to be called a Methodist was becoming more and more dangerous. The cry was now "Methodists are fanatics; they must be opposed."

George felt a terrible sadness as he read of the latest sufferings of Methodists for their beliefs. "Look here, Syms, the rioters do whatever they please and the magistrates do nothing to stop them."

"The violence grows worse," Syms agreed. "I fear what it will do to our people. Look here at what they did to young Adams."

In Hampton a mob of hundreds dragged the Reverend Thomas Adams from his pulpit, threw him into a nearby lime pit, and then into a pond injuring him severely."

"We must go to his aid," George said. When the leaders at Hampton heard George was coming, they declared him their next victim.

George arrived in town before the mob gathered. He was preaching inside the large house of a friend when the mob arrived. George stood at the top of a staircase to speak to those below him. When the mob pressed inside George leapt down the stairs toward them, causing them to run outside in a fright. Some thought he had flown down. Later George said, "I had no idea that I would do such a thing." The mob stayed outside until late in the evening ready to attack anyone who tried to leave. Adams was seized again, wounded and thrown back into the pond. Others too were injured before the rioters finally left.

George went at once to three clergymen in the town to ask for their help. "But Mr. Whitefield," one of the clergy, who was also a justice of the peace, said, "These happenings are all thanks to you, Sir, and your wild, fanatic teachings. Go home, and let the people alone if you wish to help them."

"These rioters take the law into their own hand and do great harm to those who have done them no harm," George said as he and Marcus left. "It's time we took action. We must call our people together to pray and fast. I will go before the court in Gloucester and make formal charges against these Hampton rioters."

In court the rioters claimed, "We took action to stop the fanatic Methodists for the good of the people." On George's side three of the witnesses who were not Methodists gave clear proof that the riot was not the fault of the Methodists at all. The jury looked grim as they listened, but they ruled in favor of George's side, and condemned the rioters to pay damages set by the King's Bench Court. George stood and said, "We will not ask for payment. It is enough that these men know they can be called before the court and punished." After the court case violence against Christians lessened though it did not stop completely.

George was needed at the Orphan House. "Elizabeth must come too," he said.

A Murderous Attack

The war between France and England made it too dangerous to sail. However, George found a room in Plymouth, where he could wait for a ship that would sail with a naval convoy as an escort. Elizabeth had not yet come.

George spread his letters from the orphanage on the small table in his new lodging, and read the letter from young Martha again. "Mr. Whitefield, I am so sorry to tell you this," Martha wrote, "but I fear I have not been a very good girl all this week. Mrs. Henning says she shall give me no supper again, if I do not take better care not to tear my dresses. I confess that I forgot all about my dress when I chased that old pig, Rumbles out of the garden. I think I should not have tried to ride him. Do you know, Sir, how slippery a pig can be? If I had not fallen off I would not have tumbled into the wire the gardener left by the fence so he could repair it, and I would not have torn my dress. Mrs. Henning says young ladies shouldn't be riding pigs anyway. I will try to remember that. If only I didn't forget so much. Like walking is better than running on muddy paths, the rooster will peck you if you chase him, and lots of things like that. I do ask

Jesus to forgive me. Do you think he is tired of me too like Mrs. Henning?"

George's laughter was loud enough for his landlady and her daughter to hear in their downstairs apartment. "Ah, precious child," he whispered at last, "a little girl may forget again and again, but Jesus will never stop loving you, little one." George wrote to young Martha, finished his evening work, read and prayed, and was ready for bed. While he waited for his ship he would put the time to good use and preach throughout Plymouth in the open air. Tomorrow he would begin. The gentle knock at his door surprised him.

"Mr. Whitefield, there is an officer from his Majesty's navy come to see you. Shall I bring him up, sir?" his landlady called.

"Yes, thank you, do let him come." Like many another the man was probably coming for counsel, George thought. When the officer entered he shut the door behind him and took the chair George showed him. "What may I do for you, Sir?" George asked. The man seemed to think for a little, and then stood. George did not notice the gold headed cane in his hand until it came swinging towards his head.

"Dog, rogue, villain," the stranger said with each swing of his cane at George. The blows coming down on him did not stop, and George knew his attacker had no intention of stopping them. As he fell to the floor, and tried to shield his face, he cried out, "Murder, help, murder!"

The landlady and her daughter hearing his shouts came rushing up into the room. "Stop, stop that," the landlady cried grabbing at the attacker's collar. Her daughter screamed and held on to the man's coat, but he quickly threw them both off, and went back to beating George. Suddenly a second attacker rushed into the room and pushed the landlady and her daughter out and down the stairs. But before he could join the first attacker the neighbors who had heard the screams and shouts burst into the house to help. The assailants fled out the window and across the roof. George was badly bruised, but thankfully no bones were broken. To the trembling landlady and her daughter George said, "May the Lord greatly reward your bravery and courage tonight. I believe those men meant to murder me." George wrote of the event to Marcus giving full credit to his landlady and her daughter for their bravery. No one knew who his assailants were, but now the people of the town insisted on guarding George on his way back to the rooming house each evening after his preaching in the fields. For six weeks as he waited for the ship George preached and ministered to all who came from far and near to hear the Word of God.

Sometimes George had almost no time to eat or rest. As always he rose at four in the morning to read and pray, and tried to go to bed by ten when he could. "I marvel at the hunger of people for God in so many places," George wrote to a friend.

One evening the sea of people before him stretched away far beyond the wooden platform where he stood. As he prayed a hush began to spread like waves across the sea of faces. When George began to preach, his voice reached to the very edges of the crowd, so that no one left because they could not hear. But this night someone who hadn't even come, heard him.

A young shipwright named Tanner and his friends could hear George's preaching voice where they stood, a good distance away from the crowds. Young Tanner who cared nothing for God was ready to bring this preacher down just for the sport of it. "Come on lads," he said, "fill up your pockets with some good fat stones and let's go get him." Eagerly, the others followed his lead.

As they drew near the hushed crowds and tried to press their way through, they were quickly separated from each other. The shipwright found himself tightly wedged before and behind just as George spoke the words from the Bible story in Acts: "Thou bringest certain strange things to our ears, we would know what these things mean." Tanner began to listen. The next night he returned alone, and inside he knew the preacher's message was for him. He left knowing he needed God's mercy. The following night Tanner came back again, and this time as he listened he found the mercy of God. He wrote a note to tell George of his new faith and confessed how he had come to the first meeting with a pocket full of stones and an empty heart. George read the note, once more amazed at God's work. When he heard from Tanner the shipwright years later, it was to tell George that he was now the minister at the newly built Tabernacle of Exeter.

At last Elizabeth arrived. "Elizabeth!" he cried in welcome as her coach rolled to a stop. He soon embraced her small frame in his arms, and kissed her cheek. "Now that you are here I can hardly wait to begin our sea journey. It will do us both good."

The first ship George hoped to take to America refused him. "Sir, I do not want you aboard preaching and ruining my sailors," the Captain said. When another ship arrived George felt thankful when its captain gladly welcomed them aboard.

Elizabeth lifted her face to get a good look at him. "You look weary, dear husband. I'm glad you will be on board ship where you can rest. But you know this is my first journey across the Atlantic Ocean, and I can scarce believe it! You will have to answer a dozen questions for me surely."

George laughed and took her arm. "If it is only a dozen, why then I shall be glad to do my best," he said. "I plan to fill you in with all the news coming from Bethesada, including the letters from the children. You will love Bethesda, Elizabeth, and everyone there will love you." The light in Elizabeth's eyes told him she already loved the little ones waiting for them in Georgia.

The Gate of Heaven

It was August of 1744 when George and Elizabeth set sail for America, along with two naval convoy vessels. The war between England and France made crossing the Atlantic a dangerous journey. The uncertain weather on the Atlantic added to the danger. When a sudden storm struck and one of the convoy vessels was badly damaged, George's ship became separated from the convoy for the rest of the voyage. A few weeks later an enemy ship came into sight, and the Captain called the men to battle stations. George stood on deck out of the way and prayed for God's safe keeping. Elizabeth, dressed in a plain brown dress and apron, rolled up her sleeves to help the crew make ammunition. She was hard at work, when the cry came, "They're leaving!"

Elizabeth had held up well, but now she sat down on the nearest overturned barrel. George came to help her up. "Sorry, my dear, that your first sea voyage is proving to be such an adventure, but at least we did not need all that ammunition you made." George grinned as he took her arm. Elizabeth's hands were black with powder.

Though enemy vessels were still a threat when the sky began to darken and the wind blew hard, George knew they were in for a storm, and it was coming fast. By the time they made their way to the cabin Elizabeth found it nearly impossible to stand. George assured her, "Storms like this can do much damage to a ship, but God is with us as he was in the last storm. We will pray for safe keeping of the ship and all aboard." Elizabeth nodded, and after they prayed together George left to help the crew.

The storm did no serious damage to the ship, but by the time it was over George was soaked to the skin and shivering from cold. Soon he became feverish and ill. For days Elizabeth nursed him and gave him the medicines the ship's doctor ordered. When the fever finally broke, George saw Elizabeth half-asleep sitting at his bedside. She couldn't speak for the relief of seeing him better.

When they finally landed in the colony of New Hampshire it was October. Already invitations to preach waited for George. They were welcomed to the home of an old friend, and when they at last retired to their room George lay down immediately. "My dear," Elizabeth said, "you look so pale and tired, I hardly think you will be able to preach tomorrow."

"I must try, Elizabeth. Preaching often has been a good medicine for me." For a week he did feel strengthened when he preached, but the fever on board the ship had left him weakened. All at once he collapsed.

Every part of him felt shot through with pain. From somewhere above him he could hear a man's voice say, "I fear he may not recover from this deadly illness." George's only thought was how good it would be to leave his body behind and be with the Lord.

He thought it was Elizabeth's voice that said, "So many are praying for him, doctor. Some have been praying day and night."

The fever left, but the pain did not, and George continued quite sick. Visitors came and went. George had closed his eyes but was not asleep when he heard voices from the hall talking about the "foolish mistake" that was bringing crowds of people to hear Mr. Whitefield. "He can't preach now" one said. "Yes, and some have come a long way to hear him." George's eyes flew open. In a weak voice he called the men to his bedside and asked them when he was supposed to preach.

"Why tomorrow" one of the men said. "It was a sad mistake, sir that the notice went out. You must not give it any more thought." The men left but George could only think of one thing: he ought to go, but how? He was sure he was dying, and could see that Elizabeth and those caring for him thought the same.

Elizabeth and the colonel were standing by his bedside when George suddenly cried out to the doctor preparing to give him medicine. "My pains are gone! By the help of God I will go and preach and then come home and die." To the utter amazement of them all, George sat up and soon left his bed. He felt strengthened enough to go and preach! He preached, but on the way home again collapsed. George heard someone say, "He is gone. He is so young, only twenty-nine, yet God used him to awaken thousands here and in England. It is a great loss." Tears trickled down George's face as he lay too weak to speak, and his heart full of love for God. To everyone's astonishment, including George's, he slowly began to recover. God had plans for him yet.

As George lay on his bed regaining his strength, an old Negro woman came to see him. She sat by the fire and after a while said softly, "Master you gone to the gate of heaven but Jesus say you got to go back down, 'cause you got to call some more poor Negroes." George smiled and then he prayed, "Lord, if I am to live, let it be my joy to call them." George thought about the old woman's words. He would reach out to them at every opportunity. He would write a sermon just for the slaves to explain in simple clear words the basic Bible truths beginning with the story of the Garden of Eden in Genesis. He would teach them with words they could understand. Soon many slaves did turn to the Lord Jesus in faith. Some began to sing about their faith, the songs that would one day be called "Negro Spirituals."

Elizabeth's eyes seemed to dance with joy in the weeks and months that followed as George recovered his strength. "My dear husband, I think you will soon be off and preaching again. I won't be able to keep you here," she teased. She was right! George left her well cared for with their friends and was soon on his way throughout New England preaching. As before, wherever he went God blessed him and people turned to the Lord Jesus. For nine months George preached all over New England, and now he was eager to go on to Bethesda.

George and his traveling companions were to go by horseback so that he could preach on the way to the orphanage. Elizabeth and a lady companion would journey together and join him later at Bethesda.

As they rode they were met by enormous numbers of people waiting to greet George. "This is God's doing," he said. In one place hundreds on horseback rode with them to escort them to the next town. In Philadelphia people begged him to stay six months of the year and do itinerant preaching the other six. "It is a kind offer but I must refuse it," he said. In Virginia George found people had built Reading Houses where they could go to hear his printed sermons read.

At last they arrived at Bethesda. Among the pines three miles of land had been cleared for the orphanage. The orphanage building was a grand sight, large and surrounded with a piazza and gardens. George's eyes filled with tears. By the time he had left his horse to one of the older boys, the younger children were clustering around him. George knelt and held his arms open wide. Mrs. Henning and the rest of the staff stood by waiting and smiling their own welcome. George finished hugging the little ones and stood just as a young girl ran to him, stopped and curtsied the best she could without quite toppling over. "Martha, come along," Mrs. Hennings called.

"Martha, why what a fine curtsy," George said. Leaning close to her ear he whispered, "I trust you have not been riding any pigs lately. It won't do for a young lady who can curtsy so well." Martha grinned up at him, and George patted her head. "Run along now all of you. I will see you all again later for evening prayers."

At a small table in his office George studied the accounts that James, and his friends the Bryans had spread before him. "The debts continue to pile up," George said. "Though friends send money from abroad the mail is slow and gets lost from time to time. With the death of Mr. Noble and the money we must pay back to his estate we will have to borrow just to make those payments, and find money to pay our other creditors."

George looked up from the ledgers at the Bryans. "You have kept food coming into the orphanage, dear friends, and I cannot repay your kindness."

"We love the work here, and we have prayed and studied on ways to bring in the money the orphanage must have to keep going," they said.

James now looked excited, "We think we have a plan." The Bryans nodded in agreement. "Friends in South Carolina are offering to help purchase a plantation and slaves there. All the profit will come to the orphanage. Slavery is not allowed here in Georgia, though it will be soon if the colony is to be profitable. We cannot wait for that time. We must do something now to help the orphanage. What do you think, George?

George was silent for a moment. "I once hoped to buy slaves their freedom to be educated at a Christian school just for them. If I am to own a plantation it must be a place where our laborers, though they are purchased as slaves will find freedom for their souls, rewards for their labor, and safety. I have preached that through faith in Jesus Christ, all of us white, black, Indian enter into his family. I have spoken against all the evils of slavery, and this plantation must become known for its goodness to those who work it. We will call it *Providence*." The plantation was soon purchased and became a true haven for slaves employed there.

Elizabeth had come to Bethesda, and began at once to help at the orphanage. They shared the work, laughed at the little ones' play, read together, walked together, and prayed together. "How the Lord smiles on us to give us so much happiness in him and in each other," George said.

In the months ahead George took the gospel throughout the lower Middle and Southern Colonies. "I am longing," he said to Syms, "to reach the new areas, the frontiers pushing westward." They rode for hundreds of miles as George preached and ministered.

At last the constant riding, preaching, storms, heat, and hardships left him exhausted and unable to go on.

"You must go to Bermuda where you may rest from all preaching," the doctor insisted. Dr. Shippen was America's most famous doctor, and George could only follow his orders. Elizabeth too had suffered from the fierce heat in Georgia and was not at all well. "Mrs. Whitefield," the doctor said, "will do better to stay in Philadelphia with your friends and rest there."

"We will follow the good doctor's advice," George said. "It will do us both good."

In Bermuda, George tried to rest but before long he was preaching to the locals. He would have done more if urgent letters from England had not come begging him to return at once to England. George wrote to Elizabeth that day. "My dear, I must leave on the next ship for England for urgent business there. But you must stay in Philadelphia until you are well enough for a sea journey. Come when you can. I will write and tell you more soon. Pray for me, as I for you, always, my love."

George left from Bermuda on the first ship to England. On board and alone, he breathed in the sea air, and thanked the Lord for the time to rest. He did pray too, "Lord, how I long for all the souls that sail with me." It might mean a little preaching.

To the Rich and to the Poor

George breathed deeply of the fresh Atlantic breezes as he sat on deck writing letters.

> *"My dear Harris," he wrote, "I am longing to see you, my friend. Your urgent letters have made it clear that I am needed in England. By now you have read my letter to the King which has been published throughout England. These are dangerous times with plots against His Majesty's throne causing suspicion and unrest throughout England. Those who accused Methodists of disloyalty to His Majesty, hoped to see a price put on the head of every Methodist, but our enemies are now defeated. My defense of our loyalty to the King has been well received in England both by his Majesty and those near him. Those who oppose our preaching of the good news and spread hatred for us will have to find some other way to ban Methodists. We shall have much to tell when we meet, dear brother. G. W.*

At the landing dock, George spotted Marcus smiling and waving at him. Marcus embraced George heartily. While they walked together, Marcus said, "You have come alive again, my friend. Only three months ago, *The Gentleman's Magazine* published news of your supposed death. The good news that you are alive is shouted all over London. The people are waiting to welcome you to *The Tabernacle*."

George laughed and patted Marcus's shoulder. "I'm thankful I am still here, and after we have seen the family, we must look for the things that will make for peace among us."

Marcus quickened his pace to keep up with George's stride. "You will find your mother aging but longing to see you. She is cared for and grateful for the help you have sent her."

All England knew the name of Whitefield and the wonder that he was not dead and had returned home, quickly brought invitations for George to preach. On this July day he was scheduled to speak in the Moorfields. People began gathering in the fields early and the crowds were growing. When George stood to preach he faced the largest number of people he had ever spoken to at one time. Thousands who came too late had to be turned away. As an old gentleman and his wife walked back to their waiting carriage, he patted his wife's arm saying, "Never mind my dear. We shall arrive early enough tomorrow to hear that melodious voice speak God's word to us."

George's followers began to urge him to stay in England. "You are the one the people will listen to and follow. They come from all over England to hear you. You are the leader we need to unite all. Stay with us. There is a great ministry for you here in England." Even Marcus and those closest to him began to press him to take charge.

"No!" George said. "I cannot stay in England. We must not compete with each other, but work together in love. I came to make peace." George looked at the friends and leaders around. "No, my brothers, I will go about preaching the gospel to every creature, and leave the Societies to others. I will resign all my positions as head of anything. Let my name be forgotten. I know my place is to be the servant of all so that Jesus Christ may be preached."

One of George's followers shook his head sadly. "If you will not take leadership, will you at least deny the lies told about you over and over by our enemies?"

George answered him gently. "I am content to wait till the judgment day for the clearing up of my character. You may write on my tombstone, 'Here lays G. W. What sort of a man he was the great day will discover.'"

Eager to preach wherever he could, George paid a visit to Scotland. The opposition to him from the men of the Associate Presbytery was still strong, but for seven weeks he preached to large congregations in Glasgow and Edinburgh. The weather had turned cold and windy while George was preaching outdoors, chilling him to the bone. The following day his voice was hoarse. "I must try to keep my promises to those who are waiting for me to come," he told his host. In the morning he traveled on to his next meeting, and then to the next. His struggle to make his voice heard was now painful.

"At times I cannot breathe easily," George said to the Scottish doctor who had come to examine him at a friend's house. "And I often have bleeding in my throat when I finish preaching." Scotland's doctors were known for their fine medical practices.

The doctor had finished his exam. "I will give you medicine to help with the breathing, but you must rest your voice. You may have burst a blood vessel in your throat," he said, "and you cannot continue this way."

Forced to rest, George stayed with his friends, took walks in the Scottish countryside, and wrote letters. To Marcus he wrote, "Your prayers, and the prayers of many dear friends have brought much relief to me. I am breathing the fresh Scottish air freely now, and my throat has quite healed. I believe it is time to continue my preaching here."

As always when George stood to preach he forgot all else and spoke with all his heart. He did not feel the strain as he spoke, but afterwards the bleeding did come back. "It seems to come and go," George said. "I'm thankful for the strength I am given to go on preaching, and will trust the Lord whatever comes." He finished his tour not knowing when the strain of preaching would be too much for his throat.

George returned home to England while Elizabeth was still in America. He was glad Elizabeth was not yet back, and went right to work on a secret plan he'd hoped to finish before she arrived. At last the work was done and George wrote a letter to Elizabeth. "My dear, I can hardly wait for your return. It's been almost a year since I have been back. I miss you, but I have a wonderful surprise waiting, so hurry, my dear." George smiled to think of how Elizabeth would look when at last she came and he led her, not to a rented lodging, but to the new house that he had built for her near the Tabernacle.

In June Elizabeth's ship arrived. George took her straight to the little brick house with its garden and led her like a bride through it. "I've called it Tabernacle House, my dear," he said. Elizabeth was speechless at first, overwhelmed with joy at the very first house they now owned in England.

"I shall not have to live in Wales, while you preach in England," she whispered while tears of joy ran down both their faces.

"Yes, whether I am here or in America, as God calls me to preach, you will have this home, my dear." There was a feeling of joy in his heart, or was it pride? George smiled. Maybe a bit of pride this time was okay. The house was not grand but it was all it needed to be, and it was his first real gift to Elizabeth.

At supper George told Elizabeth all the news. "I have given up all leadership positions, but the one that will not give me up: *The Tabernacle*. I am to stay as the minister but may go freely on my itinerant preaching tours part of the time. I may even return to the Colonies, and others will preach in my absence."

Elizabeth listened and smiled as he finished. "God blesses your ministry wherever it may be. I am pleased with this good plan, and a little more than pleased that you will be at *The Tabernacle* close to our home at times."

But soon another appointment was put upon him. The Countess, Lady Huntingdon, had decided to make George one of her chaplains. London was full of the English nobility, who displayed their wealth, their love for pleasure, and their social position often with contempt for those beneath them. Many went to church because it was part of English life, but many who went had little place in their lives for God. Lady Huntingdon, loved and believed in the Lord Jesus and did all she could to bring others to him. Her mansions in the city and in the country were grand estates, and she moved in high society. After her husband's death she had decided to use all her wealth and position to serve God. She began to invite small groups of people from among the nobility and wealthy to study the Bible in her home. As chaplain, George was to come twice a week to her house and preach during the winter and other times when he was in London. For George it was one of the hardest things he had to do.

He could not help telling Elizabeth. "Each time I go to the Countess's house, I go with fear and trembling, knowing how difficult it is to speak to the great so as to win them to Jesus Christ. Sometimes, I want to say, Lord, please have me excused and send someone else. And then I hear the words, 'I can do all things through Christ who strengthens me.' Ah, Elizabeth, maybe I will always tremble, but I must trust him to do his work in me. The Lord alone can open the eyes of rich or poor."

It was time for him to leave for the Countess's house, and Elizabeth held out his gloves. "I will be praying, dear husband," she said.

George arrived to find forty of England's rich and noble gathered at the Countess's house. Only a great room with wide arches like Lady Huntingdon's grand room could accommodate the wide hoop skirts of the women. Their hair piled high with added curls and puffs held all sorts of adornments, and their jewels sparkled. George marveled at the silks and brocades of both the men and women. Like all ministers of the Church of England he wore a black wool robe and the usual powdered wig. The other men wore wigs too as they did help protect against lice.

The room was full of lords and ladies, countesses and earls, all invited by Lady Huntingdon from among the rich and noble of England. As always when George began to speak he thought of nothing but the truth he saw so powerfully before his own eyes. He was telling the story of a blind man at the edge of a precipice who lost his dog's leash, dropped his cane, and lurched forward to retrieve it when Lord Chesterfield leapt from his chair and cried, "By heavens he's gone." He had listened so intently that the danger seemed real. Lord Chesterfield did not call himself a true follower of the Lord Jesus like Lady Huntingdon, but he liked to listen to George, and had often said "He is a good man."

Some who came to the Chapel did come to believe the gospel. Already the Earl of Bath, Lady Chesterfield, a close relative of the King's father George I, Lord St. John, and others had come to true faith through George's ministry. At each meeting George welcomed questions and promised to answer the letters of any who would write to him.

Late that night, George wrote to Marcus, "I do not know all that the Lord is doing in hearts at these gatherings at Lady Huntingdon's, but what I do see brings me great joy. Mr. David Hume, who writes that he doubts there is a God, has come. May the Lord make his word reach the man's heart."

To a wealthy businessman, George wrote,

I fear what is keeping you from the Lord Jesus is the Silver Dust that has blinded your eyes to the riches of Christ.

To another he wrote,

You, dear Sir, are in a dangerous place …

It was often late at night before George finished the pile of letters waiting for him to write or answer. Tonight Elizabeth sat next to him helping with the letters. When she began to yawn not once but several times, George patted her hand. "We will stop for the night," he said. "There will always be letters to write, and you, my dear wife, have been like my right arm helping me."

"Tomorrow then," Elizabeth said between a yawn and a smile. "There are letters to arrange preaching times and places and some letters on the affairs of the orphanage," she added. George nodded.

During the winter George had preached at *The Tabernacle* and nearby places when he could. He ministered to condemned prisoners at Newbury Gate, visited the sick and poor, and along the way found orphans who needed his help. He soon collected a number of orphans, dirty, hungry, unwanted street children who tugged at his heart. His plan was to take the children to Bethesda as soon as spring arrived.

Spring came bringing early flowers to English gardens and it was time again for George to leave. "I am eager to go to places still unreached in the Colonies of the Carolinas and Virginia," he said. Elizabeth would stay in England, and had come with Marcus to see him off.

"Go with God, dear husband," she said as she and Marcus watched his ship leave the dock. Standing beside him were twenty-two needy children and the staff hired to care for them. George was taking them to the orphanage at Bethesda.

Marcus waved farewell to the passengers lining the ship's rail. "God has called your husband to preach and given him the true heart of an itinerant preacher. And I think he has given him another heart, one for the homeless, the widows, the poor, the prisoners, and needy children everywhere."

Elizabeth laughed lightly. "Yes, and once he sees to the orphanage, he will preach many times and travel many miles before we see him again. When he returns I think he will be glad to give up his horseback riding for a small pony chaise and an indoor pulpit at *The Tabernacle*. I will be truly thankful for the winter days when I have him near for awhile." She smiled as they walked together back to the waiting coach.

A Fierce Persecution

George sat on deck writing letters. He was about to write another when a strong gust of wind blew the loose paper from his lap. Before George could catch it a young boy ran to where it stuck against the rail, and brought it back. It was one of the orphan children coming with him to Bethesda, a young lad of about nine.

The boy's dark eyes looked questioningly at George as he handed him the paper. "If you want, Mr. Whitefield, I could sit on the deck by you just in case the wind takes any more papers," he said.

George reached out to brush the lad's unruly red hair from his eyes. "Martin, isn't it? I like that idea just fine. How about you sit here by me and we talk? I'd like to hear more about your days on the streets in London." Carefully the lad sat next to George and began his story. It was one like many George had heard before. Tears were in his eyes as the boy finished. "Martin, may I tell you the story of the kindest, most loving, and greatest of Kings, who never turns away a single boy or girl like yourself from his kingdom?"

Martin looked up with a surprise on his face. "It ain't a true story, not for real, Sir, is it?" he asked.

George put his arm around Martin's shoulder. "It is indeed true, my boy. The truest story ever told."

Later that afternoon the children were safely with their care givers, and George sat on the deck whispering a prayer, "The children you have brought us, Lord, are a precious trust. Help me to teach them of your forgiveness, your steadfast love."

It was October 1751, and eleven weeks since they'd left England when they arrived in South Carolina. The children were bursting with eagerness to set foot in the new world of America. George could not hide his own delight as they neared Bethesda. "You will find this the happiest place on earth," George promised. "I should like to stay here myself if I didn't go preaching the good news of Jesus in places that need to hear it." Martin looked up at George with a question in his dark eyes. George patted his head. "You will like it here, Martin, and when I come back I'll want to hear all you've been doing." The boy nodded and turned to follow the others.

On a fine morning, George and his two companions left to begin a preaching circuit. "Ah, my friends, how good God is to us. The joy of an itinerant preacher knows no boundaries." From Philadelphia to New York George preached as they went. In New Jersey The College of New Jersey gave him an honorary degree of Master of Arts. George tucked it away in his saddle bag. In Boston he was asked to preach at the Old North Church, but had to be let in by a window because the crowd had packed the church before he arrived. As they kept riding northward towards Canada, the cold weather turned the way slick with patches of ice. As always George and his companions stayed wherever they could, even if only on blankets on the floor for the night, and ate what was offered. He rose early to pray and read his Bible, and snatched what moments he could along the way to write brief letters. To Marcus he wrote, "I am thanking God for his care. My strength is back, and I praise the Lord for this. Though we will not reach into Canada this time, I will have ridden two thousand miles before I finish this preaching circuit." It was time to begin the return journey southward and back to Georgia.

In Maryland, George was invited to the home of the married daughter of an old friend, Colonel Bayard. "My dear Mr. Whitefield, you will of course not recognize me, sir," the daughter's husband said. "Do you remember the little boy in London who was so moved by your preaching that he dropped a lantern from his hand?"

George smiled broadly. "I do indeed remember the incident. I wondered later what became of the lad."

"I am that boy," he said.

George embraced the young man. "I can barely believe you're the same lad. What a joy for me," he said. "You are one of over a dozen here in the Colonies who have told me of their conversions back in England. I begin to have many spiritual children."

"You do, Sir," the young man said, "and I have heard of twenty young men who came to the Lord on one of your earlier visits to America and are now preaching. Many thousands have come to the Lord Jesus in this great Awakening in America." George could not help the tears of joy that came to his eyes.

To Elizabeth he wrote,

It is January already, and I have preached a hundred times in New England alone, and many more along my way north. Now on my return south I revisit each place to preach again. You cannot imagine the vast areas here in America where there is still no witness to the gospel. In Virginia many people come fifty miles to hear the good news preached. Some of them are farmers who leave their fields to come just for one meeting. I am now on my way back to Bethesda. I only wish you were here with me. That place brings me great happiness, as it does to those who live there. These past seventeen years, my dear, we have spent more than five thousand pounds to keep it, but now our crops support many orphans for less than half that amount. I never thought to have slaves, but our laborers at Bethesda, and on our small plantation in South Carolina, grow in the faith, and each one of them is dear to me. My prayer is to reach every slave with the gospel, and their owners. They must be treated as the Word of God demands, in all godliness, kindness, and fairness.

George dipped his pen again and wrote, "Do not be concerned for my health, my dear, as I manage well these days. The illness that brought me close to death in Philadelphia has left. The Lord has healed me. The people are hungry for the Word, and I have been more welcomed everywhere than ever before. As always I am ready to preach wherever God shall send me. I look forward to the sea voyage and the joy of seeing you soon, my dear."

In May, after only seven months in America, George landed in England. A month later he was off on a preaching tour with London at its center. "At least you will be using the chaise to go about, my dear husband, instead of riding horseback, and I am grateful for that," Elizabeth said as he left.

When George returned his eyes sparkled with the news he had been waiting to tell Elizabeth. "My dear wife, you will be glad of my news," he said. "I've been offered the use of a meeting-house, the Long Acre Chapel that is right on the edge of London's theatre district. My hope is that some of them will come to the Chapel."

"That is great news," Elizabeth said. "As a boy you loved theatre."

"Yes. As a boy I gave myself to the parts I played. Thanks to the Lord, now I can give myself fully to preach or teach a Bible story. Sadly, our theaters mock all that is good. Plays are filled with godlessness, and the vilest uncleanness. I long to tell those enslaved to that world of the new birth in Christ. I begin preaching this very weekend."

Neither George nor Elizabeth knew that while they were filled with gladness over the new chapel, others were not. A protest meeting was already gathering with plans to resist all George's efforts. The meeting was packed with actors, play writers, stage hands, costume makers, managers and supporters. A wealthy theatre owner addressed the meeting, "Good people," he said, "we know what this Whitefield has done in Scotland. Because of his preaching one of the finest theatres in Glasgow was torn down. We shall not allow this Whitefield's Methodist fanaticism to do the same here in London." The crowd shouted their defiance of Whitefield until they quieted to hear what was to be done. The plan was to drown out Mr. Whitefield, break up every meeting with noise and stones, and drive away those who listened. A large platform on nearby property was for use to sound every kind of drum, bells, clappers, whatever would help make the loudest sounds the moment Whitefield began to preach. They vowed to keep up their protest as long as it took.

The protest went further. Rioters stood at the chapel door during the service and vented their rage as people came out from the meeting. Windows were smashed and large stones were flung at some of the congregation, injuring them. Those aimed at George narrowly missed him but struck others nearby.

After weeks of suffering the opposition George wrote to the Bishop in charge of the parish, asking him to put a stop to the rioting. Some were certain they had seen a few of the Bishop's own officials among the troublemakers. "I do not doubt it," George said. "The Bishop accuses me of being disloyal to the Church of England because I am an itinerant preacher and often preach outside the church. He has forbidden me to minister anywhere under his rule without a license from him, though he will not give me a license. I must try though I expect little help from him." George was right, and soon a darker threat began.

For the third day Elizabeth held out a letter addressed to George Whitefield, but with no word who might have sent it. Her face was pale as George opened the seal. "Is it another death threat?" she asked.

"Yes," George said. "This time I am threatened with certain, sudden, and inescapable stroke. I must bring this to the attention of the King who knows that we are loyal subjects of his Majesty." The King quickly commanded an official notice be published announcing, "His Majesty's reward for the finding and bringing to justice the writers of three threatening letters to George Whitefield." "At least this will discourage whoever they might be," George said.

"Maybe, dear husband, you need to leave Long Acre Chapel and go on with the work in another place," Elizabeth suggested.

"I have thought the same and prayed about it," George said. "I've found a property in Tottenham Court Road far enough away from the rioters, but within reach of most people who came to Long Acre Chapel." By November a large brick chapel was built and ready. The numbers of people who came rose quickly, and the need for more room was clear. George agreed that a new addition should be built. When it was finished he took Elizabeth to see it. "It is 70 feet in breadth, 127 feet in length, and 114 feet to the top of its dome," he told her. The new Tottenham Court Road Chapel was now the largest Nonconformist church in all Britain.

As they walked past the green field surrounding the church and the little houses built just at the edge of the field, Elizabeth stood still. There were twelve cottages, each with a small bit of garden in front of it. Her eyes filled with tears. "These little alms-houses you have built for poor widows are a joy to my heart," she said.

"These widows pray for me constantly," George said, "as you do, my love, and you know how much I need those prayers." Elizabeth could only nod. She was grateful for those who prayed for him.

George was soon more thankful than ever for those praying widows. He was preaching in Dublin, Ireland. Large congregations were coming to hear him in spite of violent opposition from fiercely loyal papists. Here as in England, Irish Methodists were being persecuted for their beliefs and way of life.

Accompanied by friends, George had gone to preach to a large crowd in an open field. When the service was over George became separated from his friends. He could not go back the way he had come, and began to make his way across the field. Insults and shouts followed him as angry papists taunted him. Suddenly a sharp stone hit his shoulder, another struck his back, and soon someone struck him with a stick. George's thick beaver hat helped protect his head at first, until someone knocked it off. Soon a heavy blow sent him reeling. Blood poured down his face. The blows and stones kept coming as he staggered towards the edge of the field where a minister's house stood. It flashed through his mind that he might die for the faith. By the time he reached the door of the house and was pulled inside, he was covered with blood from his wounds and nearly unable to stand. The woman of the house tried to help him but seemed terrified. "I fear they will break down the house to attack us all," she said.

When George felt able to stand, he said, "I will not stay, friends." As he opened the door to leave, a coach driven by two of George's friends stopped directly in front of him, George was snatched inside, and driven away leaving the rioters behind. When they arrived at the home of Christian friends George was lovingly received and his wounds tended by a Christian doctor. "I am overwhelmed with thanks to the Lord for his deliverance and for your kindness," George said. "In the morning I must go to preach in another part of Ireland. I leave my persecutors to His mercy, who out of persecutors has often made preachers."

Some weeks later he wrote to Elizabeth:

> *I have stayed in Ireland since the rioting, and I can hardly
> bear to leave, though I must. The congregations have been
> enormous. The people in Limerick and Cork beg me to stay,
> but I must return to England.*

George returned home weak and worn out. He
continued to preach whenever he could, though
suffering once again from the weak blood vessel in
his throat. Elizabeth urged him to rest. Slowly he
returned to more and more speaking, reaching out
to the areas around London. As winter came on he
wrote to Marcus,

> *I am confined now to staying in London, and preach once
> a day, and on Sundays generally three times. Thousands
> attend every evening, and on the Lord's Day many, many
> go away for want of room. Last summer with a table as
> my pulpit, and the heavens for my sounding board, I was
> able to preach three times a day to call many thousands to
> come to Jesus. How I long that the Lord will give me that
> joy come spring to preach again."*

By spring George wrote to tell Marcus that he was well
enough to do the itinerant preaching he loved so much.

From Scotland George returned to London with
amazing news. "Elizabeth, though I did not expect
it, a considerable sum of money has been willed to
me, enough to pay all the orphanage debts and more.
What a gift of grace the Lord has sent."

Elizabeth covered her face with her small hands
and wept. "You have borne the burden of debt for the

orphanage for so long, and at last it's over," she said. When she had dried her eyes with the handkerchief George handed her, she said "How I thank the dear Lord for this blessing, and for such a husband. I only long to be a helpmate to him, though I fear I'm often a burden these days." She laughed lightly and extended her hand to George who sat close by. Elizabeth had not been well since coming home to England after her long stay in America.

He patted her hand gently. "Elizabeth, you are my right hand, the best of helpmeets. I have said it before and say it again, we have been happy with each other and together in Jesus." For a moment George had a far-away look in his eyes. "Elizabeth, there is something on my heart to share with you. I long to continue preaching the gospel until the Lord takes me home, but I am also hoping to build a college at Bethesda to train future preachers and leaders." Eagerly George filled her in on the plans he had drawn up for such a college. Because of the war between England and France it had been eight years since he had been to Bethesda. "I must go soon," George said.

A Flickering Taper

On a warm, sunny day in June George boarded *The Jenny* for his sixth trip to the Colonies. It was 1763, the war between France and England was over, and he was finally on his way. For days he had waited for this voyage across the Atlantic. Sea journeys were known to be good for one's health, and he needed to rest and recover. When the passage became rough he used the time to write letters. To Marcus he wrote:

> *I am forty-eight years old now, and it seems that I've grown stouter and my body grown weaker. Lately I'm short of breath. I have little hope, dear friend, since my last illness, of much further public usefulness. Whatever I am able to do now I think will be like the last struggles of a dying man, or the glimmering flashes of a taper just burning out. But we serve a Master who will not forsake his servants. Pray for me, as I for you. G.W.*

To his congregation at *The Tabernacle* in London, he wrote:

> *During this twelve week voyage when I had breath to preach the Captain and ship's company attended each Lord's day. You will not forget to pray for this willing pilgrim, who dearly loves you all, pray that whether absent or present, Jesus may be more and more precious to us.*

The voyage was long and this time George did not recover his strength as he'd hoped. By the time they landed in Virginia word that George Whitefield had come brought crowds who longed to hear him. George preached four times, but soon his breathing worsened and the old weakened blood vessel in his throat troubled him. By the time he reached Philadelphia he was too ill to go farther. Two doctors saw to his care, and after a week George felt well enough to be on his way. The doctors thought otherwise. George wrote to Elizabeth, "The doctors will not allow me to journey on to Bethesda." It was a year before he saw his beloved orphanage. By December he improved enough to begin preaching three times a week and wrote, "I am better, though the breathing problem and throat bleeding after I preach still comes back every once in a while."

In New York, the warm welcome of the people touched George's heart and he preached often. In Connecticut George visited the Wheelock School for Indians where native Americans studied to take the gospel to their own people. He had raised funds for it and helped send its first graduate, Samson Occum, a Mohegan Indian to England to raise interest in the school. "The south is still troubled with Indian raids," George said, "and this is a work dear to my heart. The Indians need to hear the good news of Jesus in their own tongue."

In Boston the grateful citizens honored George for collecting money for them after the great fire of

1760. At Harvard they thanked him for restocking their burned library. George's heart sang, "Only you turn hearts to yourself, Lord, and I see your hand at work everywhere!"

Though he could not preach as often as he used to do, he preached to the crowds in open fields as they headed south. At last they reached Savannah and soon after Bethesda and his beloved orphans.

At once George wrote to the governor of Georgia and the members of the Council "I shall need 2,000 acres of land for a college to be built at Bethesda." After five weeks, George received word that the land would be granted! "We have the land," he cried with a shout of joy! "Now I must be off to England as soon as possible for a charter for the college." It was February when George said goodbye to the staff and children and laborers gathered in front of the orphanage to see him off. Only red-haired Martin was missing. George smiled. "Like me," he said, "you miss seeing our friend Martin standing here with you. If he were here he would surely tell you the wonderful things he is doing now with Pastor James. And I believe that some of you children will follow in his footsteps to serve the Lord Jesus." Martin, the young orphan lad George had brought from England, had left a week ago to be an assistant pastor in one of Georgia's churches.

On board ship bound for England George wrote first to John Wesley:

> *"I have taken the gospel to new places opening up in Virginia and the Carolinas," he wrote, "but I have barely begun! Had strength permitted I might have preached to thousands and thousands. John, there is room here for a hundred itinerant preachers! I am not sorry I've been poor, or despised, cast-out, and now am almost a worn-out itinerant. I would do it all again, if I had my choice."*

He arrived in England barely able to preach at all, and wrote to Marcus:

> *"I have little strength and must rest."*

In Bristol he stayed with friends and rested. Elizabeth was away in the country to rest, and by the time she arrived home she found George well again. By October he was back to preaching.

"You must come and speak in my new chapel at Bath," Lady Huntingdon wrote. George went once again to preach to the wealthy of high society. The Chapel was filled with splendidly gowned women and equally fashionable men who preferred to attend a private chapel, especially one as beautiful as Lady Huntingdon's in Bath. George prayed, and felt God strengthening him while he preached.

At home George had new help. A young man named Cornelius Winter had come asking to work for him. When George heard Cornelius' story he hired him at once. As a boy Cornelius went from a workhouse for the poor, to live with a drunken uncle who treated him cruelly. One day, at age thirteen

Cornelius heard George speaking at The Tabernacle. As often as he could sneak away Cornelius went back, happy to catch even the last ten minutes of George's sermons. He became a believer, bought a Bible, and joined a Society, determined one day to be a preacher. Already Cornelius was preaching twice a week at The Tabernacle for George, and learning much from his beloved Mr. Whitefield.

Cornelius reported to a friend, "Mr. Whitefield preaches his finest sermons at six in the morning come summer or winter, and I have heard him say, 'while you slept, this is what the Lord gave me to speak to you.' And though a thousand people might be in the congregation, he speaks personally to you. When he weeps, he will touch your heart. I have heard him say from the pulpit, "How can I help it when you will not weep for yourselves, though your immortal souls are on the verge of destruction, and this might be the last sermon you will hear."

George was glad for this willing young man who assisted him with duties at The Tabernacle. In London, besides the care of the churches, George's love for the works of John Bunyan the preacher and author of "Pilgrim's Progress" kept Cornelius busy as he helped to prepare two volumes of the works for publishing.

Though George often felt worn out, he wrote to Marcus:

> *"O that God would open the way for me into every town in England! My itinerant preacher's heart wants to be on its way to preach come spring."*

By spring George had strength enough to visit his old preaching places. When he planned to preach in Wales, Lady Huntingdon insisted that he must go slowly and travel with her household since she was also going to Wales. As so often before, thousands came and stood in the fields to hear him.

When George had been back in London for several days he received a letter from the Archbishop of Canterbury. Marcus sat quietly as George read aloud, "I deeply regret that there can be no charter for a college in Bethesda unless the school is ruled by the Church of England."

"No!" George said. "It would mean only Church of England students would be allowed to attend the school, and not one of those I call brothers and they call Dissenters. I already have the land grant. Marcus, I will withdraw my petition to the Archbishop, and go directly to the governor of Georgia for a charter. The College of New Jersey and the Academy in Philadelphia have their charters in the colonies."

"You could call it an Academy," Marcus suggested. George nodded and at once began his new plan. He hired three builders and sent them to Georgia to begin the work.

"If the Governor can see the new building going up, it may move him to grant a charter."

In August George felt well enough to take on a brief preaching tour. When he returned Elizabeth lay ill with a fever. "I fear she will not be with us long," the doctor said. "There is no more I can do for her."

George knelt at Elizabeth's bedside to pray. She seemed just asleep, though George knew it was the fever. As he watched and prayed, slowly she grew weaker, and at last she could not lift her hand to his. On the fifth day Elizabeth slipped away to be with the Lord they both loved and served. For a long while George sat at her bedside. He had preached at the funeral of his infant son, though his heart was breaking, and now he must do the same for his dear wife and companion.

Marcus visited as often as he could. One morning as they left the Tottenham Chapel together, George looked back to where Elizabeth was buried in the vault beneath it. "Six months have passed since Elizabeth's death, Marcus, and I feel the loss of my right hand daily," he said. "Lady Huntingdon has asked me to speak at the dedication of the new College of Trevecka in Wales. Will you come with me?"

"That's just what I'd hoped to do," Marcus said. "When Oxford expelled six students last year for teaching the Bible and praying in private homes, they had no idea Lady Huntingdon would build a college for them."

"We must hope for a thousand more to be expelled for living for the Lord. A thousand youths to call all who will listen to the Lord Jesus Christ," George said.

"May it be so," Marcus sighed, "but I think none will call as loudly as you."

The reception after the dedication was a grand feast, though George would have been as pleased with a simple meal of his favorite pig knuckles. They were almost home when George said, "I long to be back in Georgia. The need for future ministers in the colonies is great, Marcus. I must return and build a college to train them."

"Will you go soon then?" Marcus asked.

"If the Lord opens the way, Marcus, I will leave as soon as possible."

Farewell to England

Cornelius could not keep the good news any longer. "Richard Smith and I are to accompany Mr. Whitefield to the colonies," he told anyone who would listen. "We sail, September 4, to America! We'll go with Mr. Whitefield Wednesday night, and Sunday morning and evening to the Moorefields Tabernacle and then to the Tottenham Court Road Chapel for farewell services."

The newspapers announced that the Reverend Whitefield would be returning to America, and gave the times and places where his last meetings in England would be held. Huge crowds gathered to hear George bid them farewell. An old baker who had heard George preach as a young preacher, could not hold back his tears as George came to the pulpit. "There is a man of God we will not see the likes of again," the baker said to those next to him. "Thirty-two years ago I heard him preach his first sermon, and now I fear we will not see him again in England." Crowds came to say farewell, and weeping many said the same thing: Mr. Whitefield, now aged by illness, surely would not return again to them.

On board *The Friendship* bound for America, George wrote a letter to John Wesley.

> *Pray for this willing pilgrim, going across the Atlantic for*
> *the thirteenth time. I am persuaded that this voyage will*
> *be for Jesus' glory, and the welfare of precious souls.*

George did not know that already John had answered his earlier letter and was sending two itinerant preachers on their way to the colonies.

Rough Atlantic weather soon made Cornelius and young Richard seasick. George, who had crossed the Atlantic many times, was not. When the ship arrived in Charleston, South Carolina, George felt rested, and more like his old self. "I must preach while I can," he said as crowds gathered to welcome him to Charleston. George preached so often that it was ten days before they were able to begin the journey to Bethesda.

The first sight of Bethesda with its two new wings brought tears to George's face. The first stage of his planning stood on what was now a 5,000 acre plot of land given to him in trust for the new school and the orphanage. "We must invite the governor, the council, and the Trustees to see this," he said to Cornelius and Richard.

A dinner for the invited guests was spread on long tables in the wing that was to be the library of the new school. Hams and breads and fruits and a bounty of all sorts of good things covered the tables. For once George did not miss his simple pig knuckles. The guests were truly impressed, and as willing as George to see a fine school in Georgia. Thanks to the great sum still left from his legacy, George had money to see to the work. The Georgia newspaper wrote of the plans for "The New Academy" at Bethesda. George was confident that soon he would see the school open. The orphanage would remain, and shortly after his guests had left, James came to say, "We have just received six new orphans, all of them quite young and ready for good food and clean clothes." George smiled.

"We must be off on our next venture," George said to Cornelius and Richard as they walked in the cool air of the evening. "I love it here," George continued, "it feels like home to me, but I am longing to be off to the North, to the frontiers, to preach the gospel. The college will be fully built by the time we return."

George stood for a minute looking at the building work and nodded. "Cornelius, you have your work ready for you here." George put his hand on Cornelius's shoulder. "You are as fine a young man as I know, and I could not leave a better man for the work. Richard and I will miss you on our travels, and pray for you as often as we think of this place."

"Until you come back we will pray for you every day," Cornelius promised.

Richard, who handled the dozens of invitations that came daily asking George to preach throughout the colonies, said "Sir, where do you wish to begin?"

"We must visit first those places in Savannah, and then to Philadelphia. I feel such a fire of joy inside that it blazes up, and I am ready to preach the love of our Lord Jesus wherever he leads," George said.

George finished preaching in Savannah, and on an early morning in April he and Richard boarded a boat to Philadelphia. Here he was so known and loved by the people that the numbers who thronged to hear him were enormous. His welcome was so large that George had to preach twice on Sundays and three to four times a week. He had grown portly, and illness had aged him, but he preached with the same powerful voice as before. Many Philadelphians thought this might be the last time they would hear him in their city. Richard saw the tears he had seen back in England as people listened to the voice they might not hear again in this life. Churches and chapels were no longer closed to George. "Though I have loved my outdoor pulpits," George said, "I am most at home within the church."

His days and nights were full and George should have been worn out. Instead he felt strong again and eager to go on with his preaching. "We will need horses," he said to Richard, "for I am ready to ride and take the gospel to those who need to hear. We will head for New York in the morning." They left on horseback an hour after dawn.

It was July and by the time they reached New York, George had preached to many along the way. He wrote to an old friend:

We have ridden above a five-hundred mile circuit. Thanks to the strength the Lord gave me, I have been enabled to preach and travel through the heat of every day. The congregations have been very large and much moved. In two or three days I hope to set out for Boston. But, dear friend, I must tell you about an event that happened recently.

"A condemned horse thief wrote to me, and I wrote back. On the day of his execution I was to preach at that same place. Thousands attended and the sheriff allowed the man to come and hear my sermon. The man came to Christ and went to his death trusting him. He asked me to speak at the gallows before he was hung, and I did, standing on his coffin as preachers do at a gallows. Afterward many wept and came to seek the Lord. The day was far gone before we could leave, but what a day of sadness and joy. Well, my brother, pray for me, as I shall do for you."

In Connecticut George was invited to speak in the church of a descendant of the great Puritan preacher Cotton Mather. George stepped forward slowly and stood in the pulpit. "I feel as I did when I stood in the pulpit of that giant of faith, John Bunyan," he said. "Here is another pulpit that I stand in humbly, remembering the mighty servants of God who preached here. It is a great privilege."

Richard forgot himself as he listened to George preach that special day. George preached the message God had flooded his own heart with, in such power and joy that it filled the church and Richard's heart to overflowing. The enormous congregation listened without a sound, to what for the rest of their lives would be called "the day of wonder."

Afterwards George and Richard rode on to Boston where George was to speak. His sermon that night was on the greatness of God in creation and redemption. He was preaching when a sudden storm unleashed thunder and lightning overhead. George knelt by the pulpit, and began to say the words of an old hymn:

> *Hark the Eternal rends the Sky,*
> *A mighty voice before him goes—*
> *A voice of music to his friends,*
> *But threatening thunder to his foes.*
> *Come, children, to your Father's arms;*
> *Hide in the chambers of my grace*
> *Till my revenging fury cease.*

George stood and said, "Now, let us sing that hymn, a hymn you are all familiar with." With his great voice George led them in song. The storm passed soon, and George returned to his sermon.

Throughout the journey George had felt his old energy and strength as he rode and preached. Like the blazing up of a fire that burns brightly before it begins to fall, little by little his strength now began to fail. His old sickness returned. Richard saw him growing weaker, and urged him to rest. "All is in His hands," George said. "We'll press on."

When his breathing became too labored and he had to rest, they would stop for a day, sometimes two until he could go on to the next town. The crowds who knew he was coming still came in such large numbers to hear him, that George was forced to preach outdoors.

A minister in the town of Newbury Port had invited George to preach and to stay at his home. On the way George preached for two hours standing in a large field before a crowd. George was tired, but decided they should press on. It was late in the evening when they arrived at the minister's home in Newbury Port.

"I am weary tonight, friends," he said, "and must retire early." His host asked if he would first say some few words to those who had come to the house to greet him. George was already on his way to bed with a candle in his hand and about to climb the stairs, but he agreed. Standing on the stairs with the candle still in his hand, he spoke to those gathered below, words of great tenderness. He spoke until his candle finally sputtered out.

Richard slept that night in the same room as George as he sometimes did, ready to help if George's breathing became too labored. George had fallen asleep quickly, and Richard went to his own bed. Not many hours later, he heard George praying for the work, some of it here, and some back in England. The next time Richard woke it was to sounds of choking.

"I cannot breathe," George tried to say. "Help me to the window."

Richard had already opened the window wide. "It is your old sickness that's come back," Richard said. "We have seen it too many times lately. It will pass; it must." This time it did not pass, and George struggled desperately to breathe while Richard did all he knew how to help. When the doctor came, George had breathed his last in Richard's arms. "Surely we can wake him," Richard begged. The doctor shook his head. "He has already left us," he said. It was September 30th, 1770 and not yet dawn.

In England, Scotland, Ireland, Wales and in every colony of America, black draping signaled the death of the man who had said, "The world is now my parish." The mighty voice that had awakened a generation and preached the "new birth" to all who would listen was now praising his beloved Lord, and would never cease.

Thinking Further Topics

1. The Boy from the Inn

Why was George called Squint Eyes? Are there things you wish you could change about yourself? What does the Bible say to us about the way we were made? (Psalm 139:14–15)

George had a gift for acting and public speaking and used it at school and to entertain his friends. Do you have something you are good at? What does the Bible say about our gifts? (Romans 12:4–8) Can you think of someone who is good at encouraging others?

George prayed for God's forgiveness when he was a boy. Does God always hear our prayers? Look at Psalm 107:1–30, and find some of the kinds of people in the Psalm whose prayer God heard and answered.

2. The Servitor and the Methodists

George wanted to become a minister and was willing to earn his way through school. How did his hard work at the Inn help him be a good servitor? Do you have a goal, or something you think you may become some day? George faced lots of temptation from his room-mates to take the easy road to reach his goal. What temptations do you find in today's culture? How did joining the Holy Club, the Methodists, help George? Why were they called Methodists? How can a youth group or Sunday school help you live the Christian life in an ungodly culture?

3. Burn the Book, throw it down, or search it?
Why did this book trouble George so much? Up to now as a member of the Holy Club wasn't he living a pretty holy life? The book talked about needing God's life in us and Christ in us, and George didn't understand what that meant, but he did want to be a real Christian. How did he decide to try to become a real Christian? Can you think of religions today that believe good works will get them into heaven? What did George pray when he finally saw that he was completely helpless to help himself? How does anyone become a real Christian? (Acts 16:31)

4. A New Fire
George was eager to share his new faith. What did his family think about this new birth? What did his old friend Harry think about George's new faith? What are some of the responses unbelieving friends and schoolmates may have when we try to talk to them about our faith? God sent Lady Selwyn and Bishop Benson into George's life to help on the road to becoming a minister. Can you think of anyone who has helped you? How does God guide us? (Psalm 119:105)

5. The Voice that Awakened England

In this chapter God used two short-term ministry jobs to do a great work in George's life. Can short-term mission trips with the church be things God might use in your life? How did God answer George's prayer to bring London to himself? How did George's ministry bring real change to Bristol's terrible Newgate Prison?

Why did George say pride was sinful? Is pride ever good? Can you think of times when it becomes sinful? What should we do about it?

As George's ministry grew so did the opposition to it. Today in many parts of the world there are Christian young people facing severe opposition because they are Christians. Read Hebrews 13:5. How can knowing God's promises help us?

6. I will win them with Guile

Before George left for America he encouraged new believers to join the Religious Societies where they could study the Bible, pray, and help each other grow in faith. How do youth groups or Sunday School classes help believers today, especially new believers?

George didn't think John Wesley's casting lots to find out God's will was a good thing. When the Old Testament tells about the high priest using the Urim and Thummim stones to cast lots, they did not have all of the Bible as we do today. Who is our High Priest today? (Hebrews 4:14–16) How do we get guidance from the Lord today?

What does George Whitefield mean by "I will win them with guile?" How did George win over the soldiers and sailors on board ship? When Jesus called Peter, John and James to leave their fishing business and follow him, what did he say they would catch from then on? (Luke 5:10).

7. Thank God, the fields are open

On the return trip to England how did God use a storm to bring Captain Gladman to Himself?

Back in England when George could not preach in the churches and began preaching in the fields, how did people respond? When George raised money for the first school for Kingswood children the colliers asked him to lay the first brick. What did they say about George's coming to them? Does God want to reach people like the Kingswood people today with the good news of Jesus? How might young people support or encourage missionaries who are working among homeless and needy people?

What was the heart of George's message at Kingswood, the Moorfields and Kensington Commons? Why did so many people come to believe in the Lord Jesus?

8. The Whole World is now my Parish

When George became an itinerant preacher he said "The whole world is now my parish." How are some of today's evangelists like the itinerant preachers of Whitefield's day? Where does the Bible say the gospel has to be preached before Jesus returns? (Matthew 24:14)

On board ship when George was thinking of his many faults and failures as a Christian, he told his fears to Jesus and confessed his sins. What great advice did he give in his letter to Marcus? How does it help us to know that Jesus is our righteousness? If God has called us to be his children will he also keep us all the way to Heaven? (Philippians 1:6)

What did George say makes a Presbyterian or Baptist or Methodist or person from another denomination a brother or sister in the Lord?

9. Whitefield is Coming!

Why did the clergy of the Church of England who first welcomed George, change their minds and begin to oppose him?

When people today talk about being 'born again' do they mean the same thing as the 'new birth' George preached? Is it always popular to be known as a born again believer today?

Benjamin Franklin loved to hear George preach and thought he was a good man, but didn't take the message George preached into his heart. Do you know people like this? Who opens hearts to receive the good news of Jesus? (Lydia's story in Acts 16:14)

10. A House of Mercy

In this chapter George Whitefield faces two great disappointments, the first when he loses control of the orphanage to local magistrates, but must pay all the orphanage's expenses as well as a yearly rent. Often the work of missionaries overseas is challenged by the authorities. Sometimes Christians face challenges in schools over prayer or things like having Bible study groups. What are the some of the ways you can think of to deal with such situations?

The second disappointment was the Delamot's refusal of George's proposal to marry their daughter. This time George put aside his loss and kept busy getting ready for his spring preaching tour. Why is it sometimes best to let a disappointment go? How might working on a project help? If God is in control of our lives can we trust that he has something better in store for us?

11. A Bold Itinerant Preacher

Slavery was legal and common in George's day, but George strongly stood up against the cruel treatment of slaves by their owners. What does the Bible say Christians should do about injustice and cruelty? (Isaiah 1:17) How could we apply this to situations such as bullying in our schools? Do Christians need to take a stand for what is right?

Blessings and trials seem to come close to one another in Whitefield's ministry. The Bible tells about the life of Paul and gives us good examples of both the trials he suffered and the blessings. What were some of the great joys Whitefield had in this chapter?

An old song says, "Count your blessings, name them one by one, count your many blessings see what God has done." Why is that a good idea for a Christian to do?

12. You Must Cover your Ears

John Wesley broke off his friendship with George for a while because he believed George's preaching was not correct, but God did restore their friendship. They settled their differences as Christian brothers, though they didn't agree with each other on some things. What must Christians agree on? What kinds of things is it okay to disagree on? How should we treat others who we may disagree with on some issues? What does the Bible say? (Romans 14:1–3)

If you attended a youth group that didn't welcome others who were different from the rest of the group, what opportunities might be lost?

13. A Great Joy and a Deep Sorrow

What is a revival? How did the revival at Cambuslang start? George wrote to Marcus that this revival was like the Bible story of the Passover in Josiah's time. What happened then? (2 Chronicles 35: 6-18)

Could a revival happen in our modern world? What about the great numbers that turn to the Lord Jesus during the Billy Graham Campaigns? Can you think of others?

When George's little son died soon after birth, George and Elizabeth had deep sorrow though they knew he was with the Lord. You may have lost someone you loved through death or a divorce. Is it okay to be sad? What did Elizabeth say about her sorrow? What hope did she speak of? How can we find comfort in Jesus when we suffer grief? (2 Corinthians 1:3–4)

14. A Murderous Attack

A Naval officer and his accomplice intended to murder George, but God had other plans. What does the wicked man say in Psalm 94:7? What does God say in Psalm 94:8–9? Who did God bring to help save George's life? After the attack George continued to preach and because he did a young shipwright named Tanner became a Christian. What was Tanner's reason for going to hear George speak? How did God keep Tanner from carrying out his plan? What caught Tanner's attention that made him listen to George? How do you think George felt when he heard the good news about young Tanner? Can you think of times when some good thing you didn't expect happened because you were obeying God? Read Mark 9:41.

15. The Gate of Heaven

Preaching had often acted like a good medicine for George before but not this time. When George lay slowly recovering how did God use the old Negro woman who came to visit him? What was George's response to her words?

George made a sermon to teach slaves the great Bible truths in words they could understand and many became Christians. Do you think people today know as much about the Bible as they did in past generations? What about teens in today's culture, do they need to hear the good news of Jesus in words they can understand? Is it important to think about the words we use when we share our faith with others?

What does Providence mean? How did George turn his plantation into a true haven for his slaves? What did he mean by saying it was to be a place where they would find freedom for their souls?

In Bible times there were slaves and still are in some countries. What does the New Testament teach about slavery? (1 Corinthians 7:21–22, Philemon 1:15–16)

16. To the Rich and the Poor

When people urged George to stay in England and be their leader he said "No. Let my name be forgotten." What did he say his place was? What did he say they could write on his tombstone? What great day did he mean? (2 Corinthians 5:10 and 1 Corinthians 3:13) What did Jesus say about those who wanted to be the greatest among his followers? (Matthew 20:25–28) Does this mean that no matter what our position or job is we can still be servants in some way?

As Lady Huntingdon's chaplain, George preached to the wealthy and noble. Why did he find this hard to do? Is this true in today's world? Do people who are rich find it hard to turn their lives and possessions over to God? Read Matthew 19:23–24.

17. A Fierce Persecution

What made George leave Long Acres Chapel? After the hardships and failure there George built the Tottenham Court Road Chapel that became the largest Dissenter church in Britain. He also built twelve almshouses for poor widows next to the chapel. How did the widows turn out to be a help to George?

In Dublin, Ireland, George faced danger and persecution once again, and again God delivered him. When George said, "I leave my persecutors to His mercy, who out of persecutors has often made preachers," he could have chosen Paul in the Bible as an example (Acts 26:9–11), or Levi the tax collector (Matthew 9:9). Can God do the same for our persecutors today if it is his will? What does the Bible say we can do when we are in a bad situation and see no way out? (Psalm 23:4–6) What can ever separate us from God's love?

18. A Flickering Taper

George was only forty-eight, but felt that he was truly like a taper (candle) close to burning out. What had George spent his whole life doing? When George said

"I am not sorry I've been poor, or despised, cast-out, and now am almost a worn-out itinerant. I would do it all again, if I had my choice." Why do you think he would do it all again? How do we think of George Whitefield today?

After Elizabeth's death how did Marcus help comfort his friend George? Can you think of other ways friends can help?

19. Farewell to England

George was persuaded, he said, that this trip would be for the glory of Jesus and the welfare of precious souls. What did he feel like when he landed in Charleston? How many miles long was the preaching circuit George and Richard made on horseback? Back at the orphanage what kind of fire did George say blazed inside him that made him ready to preach the love of the Lord Jesus anywhere? Can we have that fire?

Think of some of the things that happened along the way as George and Richard visited place after place in the colonies, things like the time George preached on top of a condemned prisoner's coffin, or preached during a big storm, and tell why you chose it. Why do you think George's last trip was for Jesus' glory and for the welfare of precious souls?

What did George Whitefield's story tell you about God?

Bibliography

Andrews, J. R., *George Whitefield: A Light Rising in Obscurity* (London: Morgan and Chase), 1864.

Dallimore, Arnold A., *George Whitefield: The Life and Times of the Great Evangelist of the Eighteenth Century Revival, 2 volumes*. (Westchester, IL: Cornerstone Books), 1970, 1979.

Davis, William V., *Introduction, George Whitefield's Journals* (1737-1741). A Facsimile Reproduction of the Edition of William Wale in 1905. (Gainesville, FL: Scholars' Facsimiles and Reprints), 1969.

Johnson, E. A., *George Whitefield: A Definitive Biography. Two volumes*. (Stoke-on-Kent, UK: Tentmaker Publications), 2008.

Lambert, Frank, *Pedlar in Divinity: George Whitefield and the Transatlantic Revivals*, 1737-1770. (Princeton, NJ: Princeton University Press), 1994.

Letters of George Whitefield: For the period 1734-1742. (Edinburgh, UK: The Banner of Truth Trust), 1976.

Macaulay, Dr., *Whitefield Anecdotes: Illustrating the Life, Character, and Work of the Great Evangelist*. (London: The Religious Tract Society), no date.

Stout, Harry S., *The Divine Dramatist: George Whitefield and the Rise of Modern Evangelicalism*. (Grand Rapids, MI: Eerdmans), 1991.

Author's Note

Two names were known throughout all the American colonies in the 1700's: the name of the king, and George Whitefield's. Thousands came to hear him, often like the farmer who hearing that Whitefield was coming to preach in a town twelve miles away left his fields and ran to get his wife and horse to be there in time to hear him. Who was this young preacher that God used in what is called the Great Awakening that swept through not just America, but England, and Scotland? From his first sermon at age twenty-three, to his last the day before he died, he preached the new birth in Jesus and did so with all his heart. It was his hope he said to the thousands listening to him, "… to touch your hearts."

George Whitefield loved the Lord Jesus wholeheartedly and lived what he preached. He spent his whole life taking the good news of the new birth to as many people as he could reach. He wrote a sermon to teach the basic truths of the Bible that traders could translate for the Indians. He spoke to slaves, to the poor, and to the rich with the same love of Jesus for them all. God gave him the gift of a voice that reached not just great crowds of many thousands at a time, but the hearts of thousands of those who listened. He was the most important preacher of his times, and one who lived what he preached. All we know of him tells us of a man of cheerful temper, great kindness, clear thinking who knew the Bible well, believed God's promises, loved and felt great joy in who Jesus was and served him with all his heart faithfully. We know too that he had tender love for orphans and the poor, and never turned away anyone in need from the Bethesda orphanage, not even an old man who took refuge there. There is much more that George Whitefield did to influence his times, but as he said, "You may write on my tombstone, The great day will reveal what sort of man he was."

In the book I have put George Whitefield's words in italics to set off his exact words. In all the major events of his life I have used his words wherever I could, but where I felt the need to put them in my own words for the sake of the story they are quoted without italics. In some situations where the story requires conversation I have imagined his words as he might have said them. Though he did lead a friend at Oxford to Jesus, I have given the friend the name Marcus. The orphan boy who graduated from Bethesda and became an assistant to a local pastor, I gave the name Martin. George Whitefield loved children and loved getting their letters and writing back to them as a loving father would, but Martha, the little girl who wrote about trying to ride the slippery pig is imagined for the sake of showing how Whitefield cared for children.

I have barely touched the full life of George Whitefield in this little book, but I hope that you will come from it being as glad as he was to know and believe that truly Jesus is our Righteousness.

Timeline
George Whitefield

1714 Born in Gloucester, England, December 16.

1722 Mother Elizabeth, remarries.

1725 First encyclopedia printed in China.

1726 George at St. Mary de Crypt grammar school until he leaves to help at the family-owned Bell Inn.

1727 Brazil plants its first coffee.

1728 George's mother leaves her husband. George leaves the inn to live with his mother and sister.

1730 George returns to study at St. Mary's.

1732 Enrolls at Pembroke College, Oxford University.

1733 Introduced to the Holy Club – seeks salvation by works, health breaks down.

1735 George comes to assurance of salvation by faith in Jesus. Returns to Gloucester.

1736 Finished undergraduate studies, is ordained, preaches first sermon, returns for graduate studies. Decides to be a missionary in Georgia.

1737 Preaches to thousands in Bristol and London.

1738 First voyage to America, stays in Georgia for three months then leaves to be ordained as priest and raise money for orphanage.

1739 Sails to America and decides to be an itinerant preacher.
   The Methodist Church founded by John Wesley.

1740	Begins Bethesda orphanage in Georgia. Preaches throughout the colonies to great crowds.
1741	Back in England much opposition from John Wesley's followers. Marries the widow Elizabeth James.
1742	Preaching takes him on second visit to Scotland and Cambuslang Revival.
1743	Birth and four months later, death of infant son. Attack on George's life.
1744	Sails to America with Elizabeth his wife, George is ill, recovers and returns to preaching.
1745-48	Third trip to the Colonies, much opposition but preaches to many thousands.
1748	Ruins of Pompeii are found.
1748-51	Becomes Lady Huntingdon's chaplain.
1751	China invades Tibet.
1751-52	Fourth trip to Colonies.
1752-54	Preaching tour in Wales then seventh visit to Scotland, builds new brick Tabernacle in London.
1753	The British Museum is founded.
1754-55	Fifth trip to the Colonies, receives honorary M.A. from College of New Jersey (Princeton).
1755	Lisbon earthquake kills 30,000.
1755-63	George preaches throughout Great Britain.
1763-65	Sixth trip to Colonies, often ill but preaches and is greatly welcomed.
1765-69	Ministers and preaches in England London and Edinburgh. Elizabeth dies.
1769-70	Seventh and last trip to the Colonies. Preaches his final sermon in New Hampshire. George Whitefield's death September 30.

CHRISTIAN FOCUS PUBLICATIONS

Christian Focus | Christian Heritage | CF4K | Mentor

Christian Focus Publications publishes books for adults and children under its four main imprints: Christian Focus, CF4K, Mentor and Christian Heritage. Our books reflect that God's word is reliable and Jesus is the way to know him, and live for ever with him.

Our children's publication list includes a Sunday school curriculum that covers pre-school to early teens; puzzle and activity books. We also publish personal and family devotional titles, biographies and inspirational stories that children will love.

If you are looking for quality Bible teaching for children then we have an excellent range of Bible story and age specific theological books.

From pre-school to teenage fiction, we have it covered!

**Find us at our web page:
www.christianfocus.com**

CF4•K
Because you're never
too young to know Jesus